Wonderful English

A Treasury of English Pronunciation

Sean David Burke (ed.)

Wonderful English: A Treasury of English Pronunciation
ISBN 9798630542465
© Teabags Family Trust 2019
Sean David Burke (Ed.)
Earthside Press
South Fremantle
Western Australia
www.earthsideeducation.com
2020/08

For my dad,
Terry Burke.

CONTENTS

English is Wonderful   7

Quick Reference Guide   9

I   CONSONANTS   11

II   VOWEL SOUNDS   37

III CONSONANT BLENDS   59

IV   SILENT LETTERS   93

V   COMMON WORDS   103

References   117

List of Illustrations   119

Index of Verses   123

About the Author   131

USEFUL LINKS

Wonderful English Teacher's Book at Lulu.com
TBA

Wonderful English Teacher's Book at Amazon.com
TBA

Wonderful English Treasury at Lulu.com
http://www.lulu.com/spotlight/EarthsideEducation

Wonderful English Treasury at Amazon.com
(US) https://www.amazon.com/gp/product/B086C9ZSR5
(India) https://www.amazon.in/dp/B086C9ZSR5
(Canada) https://www.amazon.ca/dp/B086C9ZSR5
(Spain) https://www.amazon.es/dp/B086C9ZSR5
(UAE) https://www.amazon.ae/dp/B086C9ZSR5
(Australia) https://www.amazon.com.au/dp/B086C9ZSR5
(UK) https://www.amazon.co.uk/dp/B086C9ZSR5
(Italy) https://www.amazon.it/dp/B086C9ZSR5
(Brazil) https://www.amazon.com.br/dp/B086C9ZSR5
(Japan) https://www.amazon.co.jp/dp/B086C9ZSR5

The Wonderful English Colouring Book (UK spelling) at Lulu.com
TBA

The Wonderful English Coloring Book (US spelling) at Amazon.com
TBA

Wonderful English Videos on Youtube
https://www.youtube.com/channel/UCM4NwCbqOinjwhHeBCCH5OQ

Wonderful English Soundfiles at Audiomack
https://audiomack.com/we_p

Wonderful English at Earthside Education
www.earthsideeducation.com

Wonderful English on Facebook
https://www.facebook.com/englishlanguage.hub

English is Wonderful

English is wonderful, something fully evidenced by the contents of this treasury. To truly appreciate English, however, its pronunciation must be achieved. Pronunciation is important, as listening and speaking are skills fundamental to learning a language. These basic skills underpin the development of reading, writing, comprehension and cultural competence.

Wonderful English is a comprehensive tool for the identification and practice of common English sounds. It covers consonants, vowels, diphthongs and common consonant blends, with engaging tongue twisters, rhyme, song and alliterative verse. It also assists teachers in exploring common culture, values and experiences, which are usually encountered and consolidated in childhood.

The book is primarily designed for use by teachers of English as a second or subsequent language. It is suitable for both beginning and advanced students. Primary teachers, as well as teachers of elementary phonics, speech therapy and drama, likewise, will find it an enjoyable and useful reference work. Parents of young children could do worse than leaving a copy carelessly lying about.

Pronunciation is physical. It involves training the mouth and throat to make sounds within the normal range for a particular language, dialect, accent and region. Many learners find that they understand quite a lot of English, but are not immediately understood by others when they speak. It can be difficult both to conquer a sound initially, and then to make that sound clearly each time.

Wonderful English generally follows a standard British English, also known as received pronunciation (RP). Regional variants, such as American or Australian English, have, *inter alia*, some very different vowel sounds. Allowance needs to be made for local usage.

The online videos and soundfiles supplement the book. It can be a good idea to listen to a soundfile or watch a video first, and then work with the text, as English spelling is often deceptive. Ideally, however, students will find a local, native English speaker to assist them, as this book is also a repository of shared culture, and culture is best shared in person. Readers are also encouraged to look up other versions of the texts used.

To watch the videos, go to the ***Wonderful English*** channel on Youtube or use the links on each page. Each full page or section also has a separate podcast at Audiomack. You will also find everything linked at **www.earthsideeducation.com** and via the Facebook page. Please share.

Pronunciation is fun. The intention is that this work will be used in a way that is social, experiential, collaborative, rhythmic and enjoyable, with an attitude to error that is playful and constructive. Some lessons will hopefully dissolve into fits of laughter: there is a place for that in every class.

Feedback, requests and suggestions are most welcome. Contact me via **earthsider@gmail.com** .

Sean David Burke   11 November, 2019

Special thanks

To fellow mid-tenor, Colin Beasley,
who generously
cast his learned eye over the text
and
improved it no end.

Consonants and Vowels Quick Reference

Consonants [Part I] and **Vowel Sounds** [Part II] are indexed below.
Consonant Blends[Part III] and **Silent Letters** [Part IV)are arranged alphabetically.

	CONSONANTS	page	Video link			VOWEL SOUNDS	page	Video link
p	as in **puppy**	12	▶		**aɪ**	as in **I**, **ride**, **fly**	38	▶
b	as in **baby**	13	▶		**ɑ:**	as in **car**, **ask**, **bath**	39	▶
t	as in **tap**	14	▶		**ʌ**	as in **cup**, **love**	40	▶
d	as in **daddy**	15	▶		**ə**	(schwa) as in **today**, **river**	41	▶
k	(& hard c) as in **cake**	16	▶		e	as in **hen**, **said**, **head**	42	▶
g	(hard g) as in **get**	17	▶		**eə**	as in **air**, **care**, **where**	43	▶
s	as in **sister**, **miss**	18	▶		**ɜ:**	as in **bird**, **her**, **turn**	44	▶
z	as in **zoo**	19	▶		**æ**	as in **cat**, **land**	45	▶
ʃ	**sh** as in **she**	20	▶		**eɪ**	as in **day**, **rain**, **take**	46	▶
ʒ	voiced ʃ as in **treasure**	21	▶		**i:**	as in **tree**, **eat**, **ski**	47	▶
tʃ	**ch** as in **church**	22	▶		i	as in **sit**, **in**	48	▶
dʒ	**j**, (soft g), as in **jump**	23	▶		**ɪə**	as in **hear**, **here**, **beer**	49	▶
θ	**th** as in **thanks**	24	▶		**ɔɪ**	as in **noisy**, **boy**	50	▶
ð	**th** as in **mother**	25	▶		**ɔ:**	as in **more**, **saw**, **door**	51	▶
f	as in **fire**, **phone**	26	▶		**aʊ**	as in **cow**, **house**	52	▶
v	as in **very**, **of**	27	▶		**ɒ**	as in **pot**, **often**	53	▶
w	as in **water**	28	▶		**əʊ**	as in **go**, **home**, **boat**	54	▶
h	as in **head**	29	▶		**u:**	as in **food**, **rude**, **blue**	55	▶
r	as in **rat**	30	▶		**ʊ**	as in **good**, **put**, **could**	56	▶
l	as in **lolly**	31	▶		**ʊə**	as in **tour**, **lure**	57	▶
m	as in **mummy**	32	▶					
n	as in **no**	33	▶					
ŋ	**-ng** as in **ring**	34	▶					
y	as in **yes**	35	▶					

I

CONSONANTS

Peter Piper

Peter Piper picked a peck of pickled peppers,
A peck of pickled peppers Peter Piper picked.
If Peter Piper picked a peck of pickled pep-
pers, where's the peck of pickled peppers
Peter Piper picked?

Anon.

Happy Birthday

Happy Birthday to you
Happy Birthday to you
Happy Birthday dear, ______
Happy Birthday to you
    Hip, hip, Hooray
    Hip, Hip, Hooray
    Hip Hip, Hooray

Trad

Picky People

Picky people pick Peter Pan Peanut-Butter,
'tis the peanut-butter picky people pick.

1979 Peter Pan Peanut Butter TV commercial

Pen, Pineapple, Apple, Pen.

D Kosaka

Video: https://youtu.be/aalZMKl4bf8	
Audio: https://audiomack.com/song/we_p/12-p	

	Video	Audio

Pease Porridge Hot

Pease porridge hot, pease porridge cold,
Pease porridge in the pot, nine days old.
Some like it hot, some like it cold
Some like it in the pot, nine days old.

Trad.

Five Plump Peas

Five plump peas in a peapod pressed
One grew, two grew, so did all the rest
They grew and they grew and they never
stopped
They grew and grew until the pod went pop!

Trad.

Peter, Peter, Pumpkin Eater

Peter, Peter, pumpkin eater
Had a wife but couldn't keep her.
He put her in a pumpkin shell
And there he kept her very well.

Trad.

Purple Paper People, Purple Paper People,
Purple Paper People

Anon.

See a Pin

See a pin and pick it up,
All the day you'll have good luck.
See a pin and let it lay,
Bad luck you'll have all the day.

Trad.

Common Words, Names and Phrases		
people	pay	Pat
part	pig	Penelope
paper	happy	Paul
put	up	Poppy
pass	public	Perth
repeat	apple	Panama

~compare apples with apples~
~as happy as a pig in mud~
~a picture paints a thousand words~
~in for a penny, in for a pound~
~like two peas in a pod~

Betty Botter

Betty Botter bought some butter. "But," she said, "this butter's bitter; if I put it in my batter, it will make my batter bitter; but a bit of better butter, better than the bitter butter will make my bitter batter better."
So Betty bought a bit of better butter, better than the bitter butter, and made her bitter batter better.

Anon.

Bobby Shaftoe

Bobby Shaftoe's gone to sea, with silver buckles on his knee: He'll come back and marry me, bonnie Bobby Shaftoe!

Trad

One bottle of pop, two bottles of pop, three bottles of pop, (four…, five…, six…) seven bottle-a bottle-a pop.

Anon.

Rock a bye, Baby

Rock a bye, Baby, in the treetop.
When the wind blows the cradle will rock.
When the bough breaks the cradle will fall
And down will come baby, cradle and all.

Trad.

How many birds would a birdbath bathe if a birdbath could bathe birds? A birdbath would bathe all it could bathe if a birdbath could bathe birds.

SD Burke

Baa Baa Black Sheep

"Baa baa black sheep, have you any wool?"
"Yes, Sir, yes, Sir, three bags full. One for the master and one for the dame, and one for the little boy who lives down the lane."

Trad.

Video:	https://youtu.be/k2vido1wO_k
Audio:	https://audiomack.com/song/we_p/13-b

	Video	Audio

Blind as a Bat

Blind as a bat and better than a bird
Better than a bird in a blackberry bush
Better in the hand and better for you
(better for you and better for me)
Bold as brass and bigger than a barn
Bigger than a barn and busy as a beaver
Busy as a beaver and badder than a bull
Badder than a bull on a bumblebee

SD Burke

Need bigger ball bearings? Look no further than Beijing's own Balls Balls Big Balls Ball Bearing Company! Find us on Alibaba!

Anon.

Bonnie B

Bonnie B has a bee in her bonnet, a bee in her bonnet has Bon. And no-one can talk to the Bonnitybee until the Beebonnet has gone.

SD Burke

Common Words, Names and Phrases		
baby	buy	Barbara
ball	belong	Bonnie
bubble	bad	Bob
be	because	Bambi
big	but	Bombay
begin	job	Barbados

~his bark is worse than his bite~
~to beat around the bush~
~the best of both worlds~
~bend over backwards~
~bite the bullet~

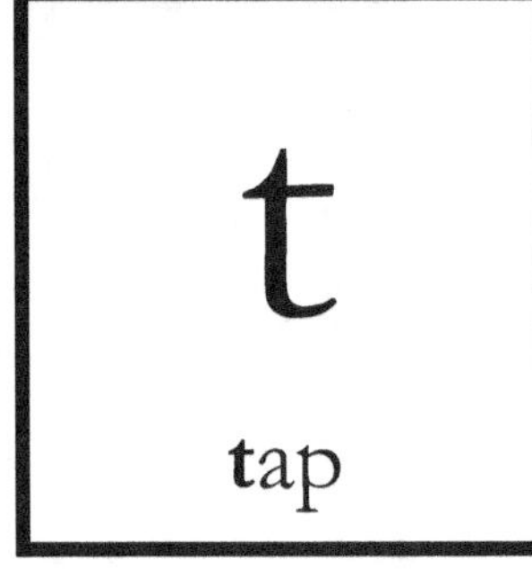

The Three Little Kittens

The three little kittens they lost their mittens,
And they began to cry,
"Oh, mother dear, we sadly fear
Our mittens we have lost."
"What! lost your mittens, you naughty kittens!
Then you shall have no pie.."

E.L Follen.

Full Kettle

Full Kettle	Made of Metal
Start to feel the heat	
Better Bet I'll	Grasp the nettle
Only fire to eat	
Pressure's on	Heat of the Sun
Moisture in the air	
Full Kettle	Made of mettle
Better bet I'll dare.	

SD Burke

Teddy bear teddy bear, turn around
Teddy bear teddy bear touch the ground..

Anon.

The lips, the teeth, the tip of the tongue,
the tip of the tongue, the teeth, the lips.

Anon.

The Moving Finger

The Moving Finger writes, and, having writ,
Moves on: nor all thy Piety nor Wit
Shall lure it back to cancel half a line,
Nor all thy Tears wash out a Word of it.

Omar Khayyam

The Tyger

Tyger! Tyger! burning bright
In the forests of the night,
What immortal hand or eye
Could frame thy fearful symmetry…

W. Blake

Oh What a To Do

Oh what a to do to die today at a minute or
two 'til two. A thing distinctly hard to say yet
harder still to do. For they'll beat a tattoo at
twenty to two. With a rattatta tattatta tattatta-
too. And the dragon will come when he hears
the drum. At a minute or two 'til two today.
At a minute or two 'til two.

Anon.

Pretty Kitty Creighton

Pretty Kitty Creighton had a cotton batten
cat. The cotton batten cat was bitten by a rat.
The kitten that was bitten had a button for an
eye, and biting off the button made the cotton
batten fly.

Anon.

One potato, two potato, three potato, four,
Five potato, six potato, seven potato, more!

Trad.

Common Words, Names and Phrases		
Tuesday	tell	Tom
time	time	Terry
table	to	Betty
take	top	Ted
teach	tall	Tokyo
bottle	together	Tahiti

~on the tip of your tongue~
~it takes two to tango~
~don't sweat it~
~let's talk turkey~
~tongue tied~

Video: https://youtu.be/J8PXbcte6Ik

Audio: https://audiomack.com/song/we_p/14-t

	Video	Audio

Ddodd

An assistant professor named Ddodd
Had manners arresting and odd
He said, "If you please,
Spell my name with four 'd's."
Though one was sufficient for God.

Anon.

Hey Diddle Diddle

Hey diddle diddle,
The cat and the fiddle,
The cow jumped over the moon,
The little dog laughed to see such sport,
And the dish ran away with the spoon.

Trad.

The Three Ravens

There were three ravens sat on a tree
Down a down, hey down, hey down
There were three ravens sat on a tree,
 with a down
There were three ravens sat on a tree
They were as black as they might be
With a down, derry, derry derry down
down…

Trad.

Did Doug dig Dick's garden or did Dick dig
Doug's garden?

Anon.

The Dame's Ducks

Heigh, ho ! heigh, ho ! Dame what makes
your ducks to die ? What a pize ails 'em, what
a pize ails 'em ? Heigh, ho ! heigh, ho ! Dame,
what ails your ducks to die ? Eating o'polly
wigs, eating o'polly wigs, Heigh, ho ! heigh,
ho !

Trad.

Video: https://youtu.be/n8gCRfI-4g4
Audio: https://audiomack.com/song/we_p/15-d

	Video	Audio

Evil Vanquished

…and the queen was forced to put on the red
hot shoes and dance until she dropped down
dead.

Grimms' (Little Snow White)

from **King Arthur's Passing**

…Then saw they how there hove a dusky
barge,
Dark as a funeral scarf from stem to stern,
Beneath them; and descending they were ware
That all the decks were dense with stately
forms,
Black-stoled, black-hooded, like a dream…

Tennyson

Where the Dwarven Dwell

Down down down in the darkest depths
Where the dwarven dwell, where the dwarven
dwell…

S.D. Burke

Common Words, Names and Phrases		
day	do	Daniel
dog	dance	Dorothy
doll	die	David
did	dark	Duncan
daddy	dead	Denmark
add	dirty	Dublin

~a good dog deserves a good bone~
~dead as a dodo~
~dead as a doornail~
~every dog has its day~
~a dime a dozen~

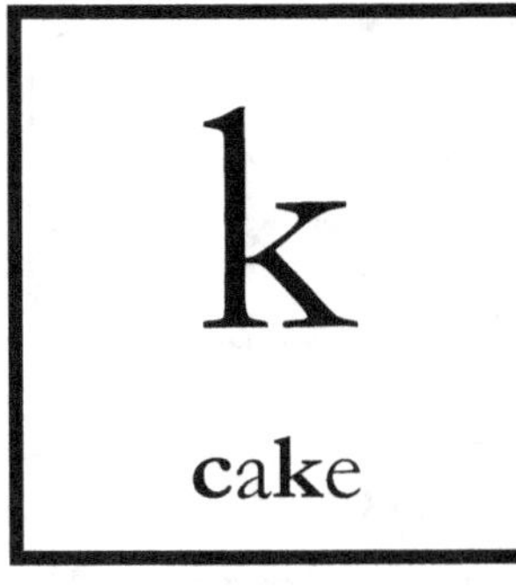

The Canner

A canner exceedingly canny
One morning remarked to his granny,
"A canner can can,
anything that he can
but a canner can't can a can, can he?"

C Wells

Hickory Dickory Dock

Hickory, dickory, dock
The mouse ran up the clock.
The clock struck one, the mouse ran down,
Hickory, dickory, dock.

Trad.

Not everything that can be counted counts, and not everything that counts can be counted.

WB Cameron

Mix a pancake, beat a pancake, put it in a pan.
Cook a pancake, toss a pancake, catch it if you can.

Trad.

Kitty caught a kitten in the kitchen.

Anon.

Video: https://youtu.be/gODAI5JQqTQ		
Audio: https://audiomack.com/song/we_p/16-k		
	Video	Audio

I Have a Dream

"…I have a dream that my four little children will one day live in a nation where they will not be judged by the color of their skin but by the content of their character…"

ML King, Jr.

Two Cats of Kilkenny

There once were two cats of Kilkenny,
Each thought there was one cat too many,
So they quarreled and fit,
They scratched and they bit,
'til, barring their nails
And the tips of their tails,
Instead of two cats, there weren't any.

Anon.

Dull, Dark Dock

To sit in solemn silence in a dull, dark dock,
In a pestilential prison, with a life-long lock,
Awaiting the sensation
of a short, sharp shock,
From a cheap and chippy chopper
on a big black block!
A dull, dark dock, a life-long lock,
A short, sharp shock, a big black block!

Gilbert and Sullivan (Pirates of Penzance)

Lock and Key

"I am a gold lock."   "I am a gold key."
"I am a silver lock."   "I am a silver key."
"I am a don lock."   "I am a don key!

Anon

Common Words, Names and Phrases		
car	come	Karen
back	call	Coco
kitty	kick	Jack
copy	cold	Eric
attack	can	Canada
can	cake	Korea
~curiosity killed the cat~		
~a cat may look at a king~		
~don't cut corners~		
~kick the bucket~		
~can't have your cake and eat it too~		

Garry McGarry

Garry McGarry, go and get your gun
Get your gun, please, Garry McGarry,
For we've got to guard the garrison
From the ghosts and ghouls
and the garish ones
So go get your gun, please, Garry McGarry.

SD. Burke

This Little Piggy

This little piggy went to market.
This little piggy stayed home.
This little piggy had roast beef,
This little piggy had none.
And this little piggy was a wee little piggy, and
he went wee wee wee wee wee all the way
home.

Trad.

Give Me Blessings

Give me blessings. Give me praise
Give me long hot summer days
Give me peace. Give me rest.
Give me nothing but the best
But if you would that I were free
Give me nought but honesty.

SD Burke

Betty Pringle's Pig

Did you not hear of Betty Pringle's pig ?
It was not very little, nor yet very big ;
The pig sat down upon a dunghill,
And then poor piggy he made his will…

Trad.

Giddy Goat

Giddy kiddy goat,
Giddy kiddy goat,
Giddy, giddy, giddy, giddy, giddy, kiddy goat.

Anon.

To Market

To market, to market, to buy a fat pig
Home again, home again, jiggety jig.
To market, to market to buy a fat hog,
Home again, home again, jiggety jog.

Trad.

How much is that doggie in the window?

How much is that doggie in the window?
The one with the waggly tail
How much is that doggie in the window?
I do hope that doggie's for sale…

B Merrill

Snug as a bug in a rug.

Trad.

Common Words, Names and Phrases		
egg	give	Gary
game	forgive	Gabrielle
garden	go	Gordon
girl	good	Gwen
get	guess	Ghana
forget	wriggly	Guatemala

~give as good as you get~
~good for the goose, good for the gander~
~your guess is as good as mine~
~it gets your goat~
~give up the ghost~

S
sister

Sea Fever
I must go down to the seas again, to the lonely sea and the sky, and all I ask is a tall ship
and a star to steer her by.
And the wheel's kick, and the wind's song,
and the white sail's shaking, and a grey mist
on the sea's face, and a grey dawn breaking…

J Masefield

A Sailor Went to Sea
A sailor went to sea sea sea
To see what he could see see see,
But all that he could see see see
Was the bottom of the deep blue - sea sea.

Trad.

Sunrise, sunset. Sunrise, sunset.

S Harnick,

Circle Song
Circles within circles here, circles with the
best of cheer. And no circle is complete 'til
the last has found his seat. While I wait to see
what will; am I ready? am I still?

SD Burke

…sidewalk social scientist don't get no satis-
faction from your cigarette…

J Destri

Video: https://youtu.be/k97LBDez1eo
Audio: https://audiomack.com/song/we_p/18-s

Video	Audio

Simon says
Simon says touch your toes, Simon says touch
your nose, Touch your head –No!

Trad.

An Earthly Hand
Well, the Earth and I are whirling in a
whoops-a-daisy dance,
And I sometimes think I'd like to stop, just
given half a chance.
And surely the One Sun of Light should have
some say in this,
A day's full revolution's not some merely
evening's kiss.
Yet somehow spun becomes the sun, and it's
much the same for me.
Just like a tired seagull is reflected in the sea,
Then wheeling down eventually to slumber in
the sand,
The dancer can reach out at will, and find an
earthly hand.

SD Burke

Sally go 'round the sun
Sally go 'round the sun, Sally go 'round the
moon, Sally go 'round the chimney tops on a
Saturday afternoon…

Trad.

Restless, hissing tongues, deliciously ambi-
tious, rapturously tasting life. I am fire.

A Albuquerque

Common Words, Names and Phrases		
Sunday	sit	Sophia
stone	sad	Sam
say	some	Susan
see	sell	Simon
save	send	Sydney
seem	set	Sudan
~better safe than sorry~		
~nothing succeeds like success~		
~S.O.S.: save our souls~		
~a sight for sore eyes~		
~dress to impress~		

Fuzzy Wuzzy

Fuzzy Wuzzy was a bear, Fuzzy Wuzzy had
no hair, Fuzzy Wuzzy wasn't fuzzy was he?

Anon.

Zachary the Dinosaur

Zachary the dinosaur,
gizzards dripping from his jaws.
Zachary the chimpanzee,
lazily hanging from a tree.
Zachary the crazy wizard;
kazoom! and Zac's sister's a lizard.
Zachary has a bloodied nose,
two grazed knees and purple toes
Zac plays and plays for days and days
-and can't wait for the holidays!

SD Burke

Too Wise

2YsUR	(Too wise you are
2YsUB	Too wise you be
ICUR	I see you are
2Ys4Me	Too wise for me)

Anon.

Going to the Zoo

We're all going to the zoo tomorrow,
zoo tomorrow, zoo tomorrow
We're all going to the zoo tomorrow
We can stay all day
    We're going to the zoo, zoo, zoo
    How about you, you, you?
    You can come too, too, too
    We're going to the zoo, zoo, zoo

Tom Paxton

Scissors sizzle, thistles sizzle.

Anon.

Y's a crooked letter and Z's no better.

Anon.

Nose, Nose, Jolly Red Nose

Nose, nose, jolly red nose.
And who gave thee this jolly red nose?
Cinnamon, ginger, nutmeg, and cloves,
And they gave me this jolly red nose.

Trad.

Busy buzzing bumble bees.

Anon.

Lazy Zvesdan

Zvesdan never did anything
He was a lazy baboon
He died at the table
As although quite able
Was too lazy to pick up his spoon

SD Burke

Early to bed, early to rise, makes a man
healthy, wealthy and wise.

Trad.

Common Words, Names and Phrases		
zoo	was	Zoe
zebra	his	Zachary
zip	zoom	Isabelle
is	zany	Lizzie
as	dizzy	Zaire
lose	crazy	Zimbabwe

~it never rains but it pours~
~easier said than done~
~he who pays the piper calls the tune~
~a nod is as good as a wink~
~use it or lose it~

Video: https://youtu.be/kS6h-BHKA24
Audio: https://audiomack.com/song/we_p/19-z

Video	Audio

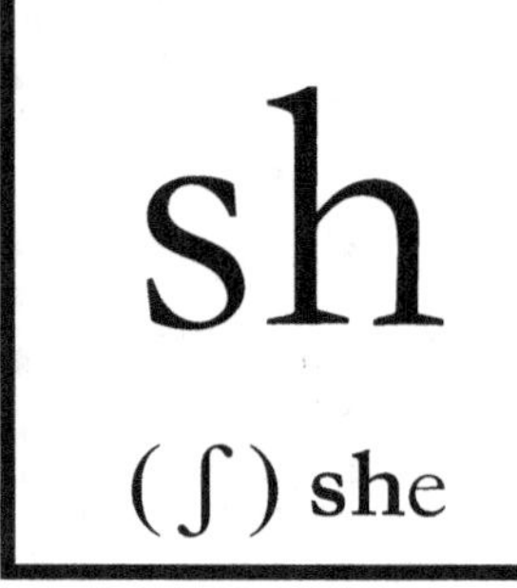

sh
(ʃ) she

Shoo, Fly
Shoo, fly, don't bother me
Shoo, fly, don't bother me
Shoo, fly, don't bother me
I don't want your company

T Brigham Bishop

She Sells Sea Shells
…She sells sea shells on the sea shore
The shells she sells are sea shells, I'm sure
For if she sells seashells on the seashore,
Then I'm sure she sells seashore shells…

T Sullivan

A dish of fish is both nutritious and delicious.
Send me some more delicious dishes of fish.

SD Burke

I like selfless shellfish, not selfish shellfish.

SD Burke

The sixth sick sheik's sixth sheep's sick.

Anon.

Shortning bread
Mama's little baby loves shortnin' shortnin'
Mama's little baby loves shortnin' bread..

Trad.(USA)

Video: https://youtu.be/HNfNEt5s-tk	
Audio: https://audiomack.com/song/we_p/20-sh	
	Video	**Audio**

The Fisher Named Fischer
A foolish young fisher named Fischer
once fished for some fish in a fissure.
'til a fish with a grin,
pulled the fisherman in.
Now they're fishing the fissure for Fischer.

Anon.

Where Are You Going To?
…"I'm going a-milking, Sir", she said, "Sir,"
she said, "Sir," she said, "I'm going a-milking,
Sir," she said….

Trad.

You are my Sunshine
You are my sunshine, my only sunshine
You make me happy, when skies are grey
You'll never know, Dear, how much I love
you. Please don't take my sunshine away

The Rice Brothers or O Hood

I Wish
I wish to wish the wish you wish to wish, but
if you wish the wish the witch wishes, I won't
wish the wish you wish to wish.

Anon

Wash the dishes dry the dishes turn the dishes
over…

Trad.

The Shropshire South Sheep Association.

Anon.

Common Words, Names and Phrases		
action	show	Joshua
finish	shut	Shirley
push	sharp	Charlotte
shall	short	Ashley
share	shake	Shanghai
wish	should	Shetland Is.

~don't drink champagne on beer money~
~give the cold shoulder~
~share and share alike~
~all ship shape~
~shape up or ship out~

The Measure of Treasure

We measure our treasures by counting each
bit.
Any subjective measure brings accountants
displeasure; double entry abjures any leisurely
fit.
But if leisure and pleasure are truer measures
of treasure then how on earth can we ever
hope to measure it?

SD Burke

Huck and Tom

"Where shall we dig?" asked Huck,
"where shall we dig for the treasure?"
"Most anywhere," answered Tom, and so they
did at their leisure
And a great treasure of gold they found
And indeed they found it under the ground
For those who toil more than they rest
Will always find their treasure chest

SD Burke after M Twain

Post Asia

There isn't any Asia;
It isn't really there.
Geographic dysplasia!
How was it ever fair
To lump almost half the world
From Turkey to Japan
In one enormous basket
Full of 'Asian Man' ?
There isn't any Asia,
Asia's not a useful place,
nor even any Asians,
just peoples in each case.

SD Burke

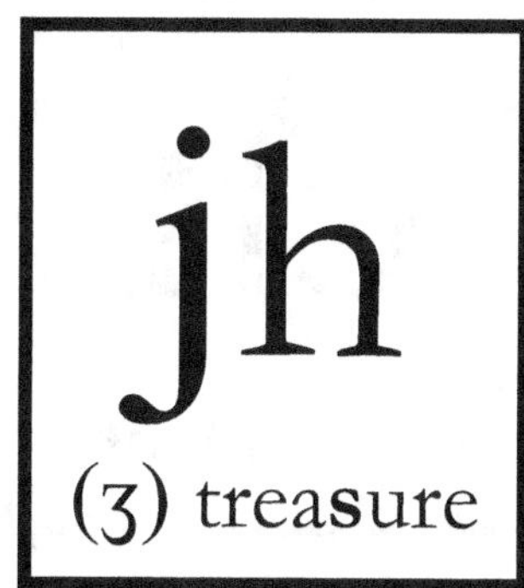

from Climbing over Rocky Mountains

…Let us gaily tread the measure,
Make the most of fleeting leisure,
Hail it as a true ally,
Though it perish by-and-by.
   Hail it as a true ally,
      Though it perish by-and-by.
Every moment brings a treasure
Of its own especial pleasure;
Though the moments quickly die,
Greet them gaily as they fly…

Gilbert and Sullivan (Pirates of Penzance)

From Kubla Khan

In Xanadu did Kubla Khan
A stately pleasure-dome decree :
Where Alph, the sacred river, ran
Through caverns measureless to man
Down to a sunless sea…

S Coleridge

Casual clothes are provisional for leisurely
trips across Asia.

Anon.

Common Words, Names and Phrases		
treasure	pleasure	Zsa Zsa
invasion	vision	Ambrosia
genre	usual	Gigi
measure	beige	Anastasia
precision	azure	Asia
collision	leisure	Persia

~one man's trash is another man's treasure~
~one of life's little pleasures~
~to have the measure of someone~
~invasion of privacy~
~the usual suspects~

Video: https://youtu.be/xkFwMcDTNns	
Audio: https://audiomack.com/song/we_p/21-zh	
Video	Audio

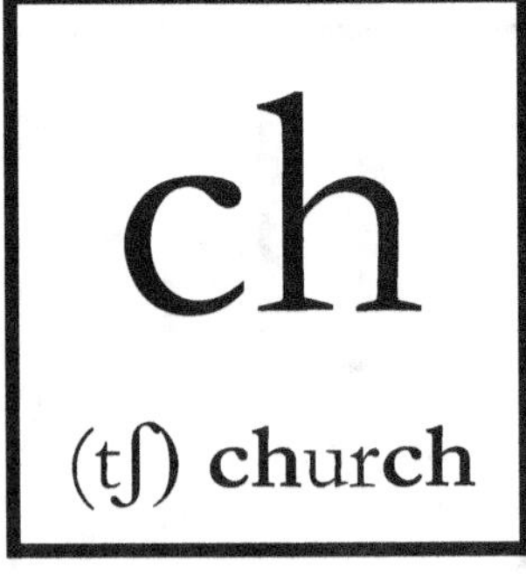

The Woodchuck

How much wood would a woodchuck chuck
if a woodchuck could chuck wood?
A woodchuck would chuck all he could chuck
if a woodchuck could chuck wood.

RH Davis

from **The Farmer in the Dell**

…The mouse takes the cheese, the mouse
takes the cheese, heigh ho the derry-oh the
mouse takes the cheese
The cheese stands alone, the cheese stands
alone, heigh-ho the derry-oh, the cheese
stands alone.

Trad.

The Witches

If two witches would watch two watches,
which witch would watch which watch?

Anon.

The best chips are fish and chip shop chips.
Fish and chip shop chips are the best chips.

SD Burke

Monday's Child

Monday's child is fair of face
Tuesday's child is full of grace
Wednesday's child is full of woe
Thursday's child has far to go
Friday's child is loving and giving
Saturday's child works hard for a living
But the child who is born on the Sabbath day
Is bonny and blithe and good and gay.

Trad.

Firenze.

Firenze! Child of beauty. A place where churls
cheat foreigners mercilessly, with a church on
every street.

SD Burke

Watchers Watching

Out in the pasture the nature watcher watches
the catcher. While the catcher watches the
pitcher who pitches the balls. Whether the
temperature's up or whether the temperature's
down, the nature watcher, the catcher and the
pitcher are always around. The pitcher pitches, the catcher catches and the watcher
watches. So whether the temperature rises or
whether the temperature falls the nature
watcher just watches the catcher who's watching the pitcher who's watching the balls.

Anon.

If a body met a body in a field of fitches,
could a body tell a body where a body itches?

Trad.

Common Words, Names and Phrases		
church	choose	Charlie
chicken	catch	Archie
children	cheap	Sachin
child	cheeky	China
achieve	chubby	Chester
teach	touch	Chattanooga

~don't count your chickens
before they hatch~
~chew the fat~
~check it out~
~children are a poor man's riches~
~who watches the watchers?~

Video: https://youtu.be/XbLql0WuSxg

Audio: https://audiomack.com/song/we_p/22-ch

Jack and Jill

Jack and Jill went up the hill
To fetch a pail of water
Jack fell down and broke his crown
And Jill came tumbling after…

Trad.

Joshua fought the battle of Jericho, Jericho,
Jericho. Joshua fought the battle of Jericho
and the walls came tumbling down.

Trad.

Jenny Who?

Jenny jumped out of the gym
And kissed me firmly near my chin
"Jeremy," she said, "it's me"
 "It's Jenny!"
    And I just stood
    And she just stared, then quietly to the
    gym repaired,
    Yes, Jenny kissed me; strange, because
    I still don't know who Jenny was.

SD Burke (after L Hunt)

The Gypsies

My mother said I never should
Play with the gypsies in the wood

Trad.

The jaunting gypsies, the jesting gypsies
The jaunting, jesting, juggling gypsies
The gentle gypsies, the generous gypsies
The gentle, generous, banjo-playing gypsies
The gentle, jesting, jaunting, juggling, gener-
ous, jolly, banjo-playing gypsies.

SD Burke

Jim Along Josie

Hey Jim along, Jim along Josie
Hey Jim along, Jim along Jo…

E Harper

Can you imagine an imaginary menagerie
manager imagining managing an imaginary
menagerie?

Anon.

Georgie Porgie

Georgie Porgie, pudding and pie
Kissed the girls and made them cry
When the boys came out to play
Georgie Porgie ran away

Trad.

Jack Be Nimble

Jack be nimble, Jack be quick
Jack jumped over the candlestick

Trad.

Common Words, Names and Phrases		
bridge	joke	Genevieve
genius	generous	Jodie
jail	gentle	John
jump	just	George
judge	jest	Japan
giant	gypsy	Jakarta

~judge not, lest you be judged~
~be just before you are generous~
~the thin edge of the wedge~
~one bridge too far~
~a gentle giant~

Video: https://youtu.be/N3pTmvdEQv8
Audio: https://audiomack.com/song/we_p/23-j

Video	Audio

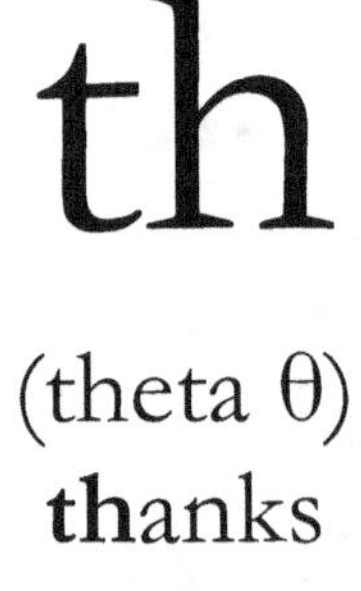

th

(theta θ)
thanks

I Hear Thunder

I hear thunder, I hear thunder,
Hark, don't you? Hark, don't you?
Pitter patter raindrops, pitter patter raindrops,
I'm wet through, so are you.

Anon.

Thousands

The thousand parts that make up my brain
Are scattered into thousands of pieces again
And amidst the chaos of a thousand screams
Fly thousands of fragments of thousands of
dreams

SD Burke

The Thought I Thought

I thought a thought. But the thought I
thought wasn't the thought I thought I
thought. If the thought I thought I thought
had been the thought I thought, I wouldn't
have thought so much.

Anon.

Nothing is worth thousands of deaths.

Anon.

Thelma's tooth's loose, Ruth.

C Beasley

Video: https://youtu.be/NCzFcqW_nP0
Audio: https://audiomack.com/song/we_p/24-theta

	Video	Audio

Thoughts Are Birds

Thoughts are birds and birds have wings and
fly
And sometimes I think a funny thought
And I laugh
And then I can't remember why
It doesn't matter
I never mind
Thoughts come back
Birds are kind.

SD Burke

I think I'd like three drops of drink

(I think I'd like three thousand, three hundred
and thirty three drops of drink…)

SD Burke

Elizabeth's birthday is on the third Thursday
of this month.

Anon.

Every day's a little death
Every thought, every breath

SD Burke

North Perth, East Perth, South Perth, West
Perth.

Anon.

For a Bride

Something old, something new, something
borrowed, something blue.

Trad.

Common Words, Names and Phrases		
Thursday	throw	Matthew
thunder	thank	Beth
thing	thin	Gareth
teeth	third	Theo
birth	bath	Ethiopia
think	moth	Perth

~through thick and thin~
~all thumbs~
~set a thief to catch a thief~
~thorn in my side~
~truth and roses both have thorns~

The House that Jack Built

This is the house that Jack built.
This is the malt
That lay in the house that Jack built….
…This is the farmer sowing the corn,
That kept the cock that crowed in the morn.
That waked the priest all shaven and shorn,
That married the man all tattered and torn,
That kissed the maiden all forlorn,
That milked the cow with the crumpled horn,
That tossed the dog,
That worried the cat,
That killed the rat,
That ate the malt
That lay in the house that Jack built.

Trad.

Whether the Weather

Whether the weather be cold
Or whether the weather be hot
Whether the weather be fine
 Or whether the weather be not
We'll weather the weather
 Whatever the weather
Whether we like it or not

Anon.

Polonius to Laertes

…This above all: to thine own self be true, and it must follow, as the night the day, thou canst not then be false to any man…

Shakespeare

Red leather, yellow leather.

Anon.

Brother from another mother.

Anon

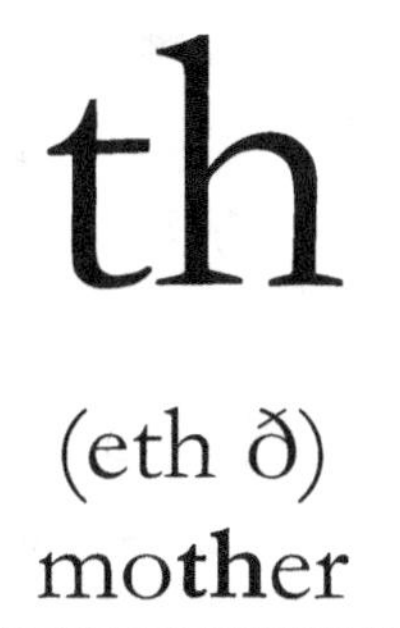

th
(eth ð)
mother

Close Family

The Smothers brothers' father's mother's brothers are the Smothers brothers' mother's father's other brothers.

Anon.

Say This

Say this sharply, say this sweetly,
Say this shortly, say this softly.
Say this sixteen times in succession.
(this, this, this, this…)

Anon.

Cut Thistles in May

Cut thistles in May, they'll grow in a day;
Cut them in June, that is too soon;
Cut them in July, then they will die.

Trad.

Common Words, Names and Phrases		
mother	then	Heather
their	bathe	Brother
this	bother	Rutherford
they	weather	The Gap
them	together	Netherlands
there	either	Wetherby

~birds of a feather flock together~
~he that speaks, sows, and he who holds his peace, gathers~
~necessity is the mother of invention~
~fair weather friend~

Video: https://youtu.be/iNRFfDUikSg	
Audio: https://audiomack.com/song/we_p/25-eth	
Video	Audio

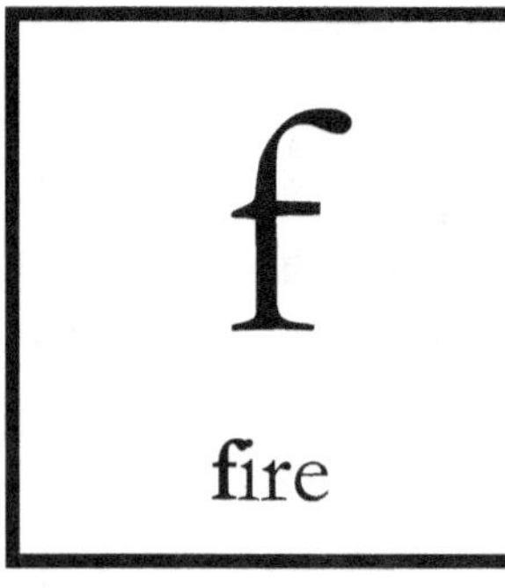

f

fire

"Fee Fie Fo Fum, I smell the blood of an Englishman…"

Trad. (Jack and the Beanstalk)

Not the Cough

It's not the cough that carries you off, it's the coffin they carry you off in!

Anon.

The Elephone

Once there was an elephant who tried to use the telephant
No! No! I mean an elephone who tried to use the telephone.

LE Richards

Lovers

From forth the fatal loins of these two foes;
A pair of star-cross'd lovers take their life.

Shakespeare

If you go for a gopher a gopher will go for a gopher hole.

Anon.

Full fathom five thy father lies.

Shakespeare

Video: https://youtu.be/1PuWCGDiMRk

Audio: https://audiomack.com/song/we_p/26-f

	Video	Audio

"Four score and seven years ago our fathers brought forth on this continent a new nation…"

A Lincoln (Gettysburg)

Little Miss Muffett

Little Miss Muffett sat on a tuffet
Eating her curds and whey
Along came a spider and sat down beside her
And frightened Miss Muffett away

Trad.

On Forgiveness

Forgiveness forms a firm foundation for future fortitude.

J Henson

East Fife: Four, Forfar: Five.

Scottish Second Division 1963/4

The Felt I Felt

Of all the felt I ever felt,
I never felt a piece of felt
which felt as fine as that felt felt,
when first I felt that felt hat's felt.

Anon.

Come Follow

Come, follow, follow, follow, follow follow, follow me.
Whither shall I follow, follow, follow, whither shall I follow, follow thee?...

Trad.

Common Words, Names and Phrases		
fire	find	Felix
phone	feel	Phillip
father	fight	Jeffrey
fish	for	Daphne
off	fat	Finland
laugh	fast	Philippines
~a fair face may hide a foul heart~		
~a fool at forty is a fool indeed~		
~birds of a feather flock together~		
~as fit as a fiddle~		
~to fiddle while Rome burns~		

The Valiant Venusians

The valiant Venusians
in their v-necked skivvies,
Voyaging from Venus
to the fringes of the 'Verse,
Vapourising vampires
and various of the craven,
Visiting their vengeance
on the evil and the worse.
Virtuous and heavenly,
their vanadium-clad cavalry
Ridding every vortex
of its vermin and its vice,
Returning home victorious,
venerable, vainglorious
-and the v-necked skivvies are very nice.

SD Burke

Five of Seven

Five lots of Seven is thirty five
Seven of eleven is seventy seven
But five of seven of eleven I fear
Is more than a little vexing
And I have no idea

SD Burke

The Happy Wanderer

I love to go a-wandering,
Along the mountain track,
And as I go, I love to sing,
My knapsack on my back.
Val-deri,Val-dera,
Val-deri,
Val-dera-ha-ha-ha-ha-ha
Val-deri,Val-dera.
My knapsack on my back.

F Sigismund & A Mazy

| Video: https://youtu.be/jP-r5r7GDDE |
| Audio: https://audiomack.com/song/we_p/27-v |

Video	Audio

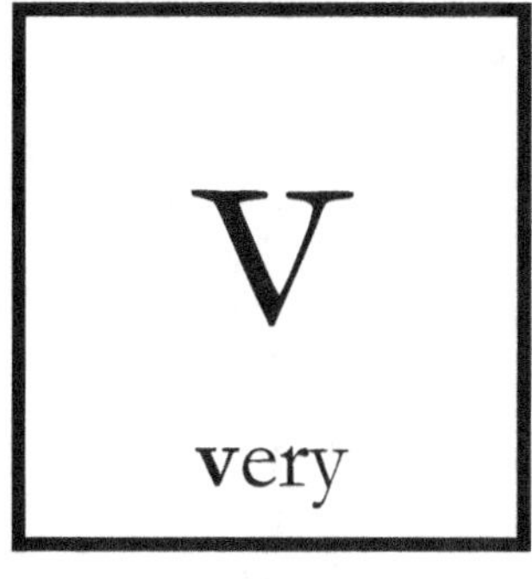

St Ives

As I was going to St Ives, I met a man with
seven wives. Each wife had seven sacks, each
sack had seven cats, each cat had seven kits.
Kits, cats, sacks, wives…how many were going to St Ives?

Trad.

Over and over the dog went to Dover.

Trad.

Ivan's Wives

Ivan's wives
-always rivals.
Armed with knives
for survival.
Five abreast,
They attack the hive,
Viciously.
Ivan's wives.

SD Burke

Common Words, Names and Phrases		
valley	visit	Vanessa
village	vote	Vincent
voice	very	Verity
of	vast	Oliver
have	vital	Vietnam
every	over	Venezuela
~play the devil's advocate~ ~fortune favours the brave~ ~every day in every way I'm getting better and better~ ~forgiveness is divine~ ~even Stevens~		

water

One One was a Racehorse

One One was a racehorse
Two Two was one too
One One won one race
Two Two won one too
(11 was a racehorse, 22 was 1 2,
1111 race, 22112).

Anon.

Why Willy?

Why do you cry, Willy?
Why do you cry?
Why Willy?
Why Willy?
Why Willy, why?

Anon.

The Water

The water flows over me,
The water flows through me,
The water dissolves the salt from my body,
The water takes away the tears from my mind,
The water fills me up,
The water cleanses my world soul.

SD Burke

Here we go 'round the mulberry bush

…This is the way we wash our hands,
Wash our hands, wash our hands,
This is the way we wash our hands
So early in the morning…

Trad.

Oh what a tangled web we weave when first
we practice to deceive

W Scott

If two witches would watch two watches,
which witch would watch which watch?

Anon.

Will you, William? Will you, William? Will
you, William? Can't you, don't you, won't you,
William?

Anon.

World wide web

T Berners-Lee

Where has my little dog gone?

Oh where, oh where
Has my little dog gone?
Oh where, oh where can he be?
With his ears cut short
And his tail cut long
Oh where, oh where can he be?

S Winner

Common Words, Names and Phrases		
water	walk	Willow
what	work	Wayne
week	wet	William
woman	when	Walter
wait	watch	Washington
wash	wear	Wagga- Wagga

~you never miss the water
'til the well runs dry~
~it won't hold water~
~wear out your welcome~
~a word to the wise~
~who watches the watchers?~

Video: https://youtu.be/vIMVvZyyz70	
Audio: https://audiomack.com/song/we_p/28-w	

	Video	Audio

A Fella

Once a fella met a fella in a field of beans.
Said a fella to a fella, "If a fella asks a fella, can
a fella tell a fella what a fella means?"

Anon.

I really like, really little, really rolly lollies.
(I really, really, really like, really, really…)

SD Burke

Little red lorry, little yellow lorry.

Anon.

Willy's real rear wheel

Anon.

Polly Wolly Doodle

Oh, I went down South for to see my Sal
Sing Polly wolly doodle all the day
My Sal, she is a spunky gal
Sing Polly wolly doodle all the day….

Trad. (USA)

Polly Put the Kettle On

Polly put the kettle on, Polly put the kettle on,
Polly put the kettle on, we'll all have tea…

Trad.

Lavender's blue

Lavender's blue, dilly dilly, lavender's green
When I am king dilly dilly, you'll be my
queen..

Trad.

The Little Laugh

A smile is like a little laugh, a little laugh is
like a smile. Especially laughs and smiles in
China, for miles and miles and miles.

SD Burke

Video: https://youtu.be/NRs0_5wpEms	
Audio: https://audiomack.com/song/we_p/31-1	

Mary Had a Little Lamb

Mary had a little lamb, little lamb, little lamb.
Mary had a little lamb, its fleece was white as
snow…

Trad.

The Pieman

I'd like to be a pieman, and ring a little bell,
Calling out, "Hot pies! Hot pies to sell!"
Apple-pies and Meat-pies, Cherry-pies as well,
Lots and lots and lots of pies – more than you
can tell. Big, rich Pork-pies! Oh, the lovely
smell! But I wouldn't be a pieman if …
I wasn't very well. Would you?

CJ Dennis

From **The Soldier**

He is that lance that lies as hurled
That lies unlifted now, come dew, come rust,
But still lies pointed as it ploughed the dust…

R Frost

Common Words, Names and Phrases		
listen	like	Ella
ball	little	Lily
well	all	Lucy
land	long	Delilah
lay	will	London
lead	kill	Liberia

~look before you leap~
~live and let live~
~feel like a million dollars~
~lucky in cards, unlucky in love~
~he who laughs last laughs loudest~

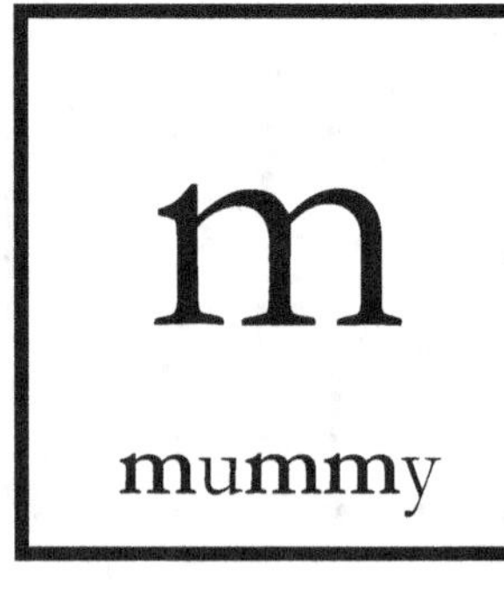

mummy

The Muffin Man

Oh, do you know the muffin man,
The muffin man, the muffin man,
Do you know the muffin man,
Who lives in Drury Lane-oh?
　　Oh, yes, I know the muffin man,
　　The muffin man, the muffin man,
　　Yes, I know the muffin man,
　　Who lives in Drury Lane-oh.

Trad.

Copper Bottom?

"Are you copper-bottoming them, my man?"
"No, I'm aluminiuming 'em, Mum"

Anon

Mo Mi Mo

Mo mi mo me send me a toe,
Me me mo mi get me a mole
Mo mi mo me send me a toe,
Fe me mo mi get me a mole,
Mister kister feet so sweet,
Mister kister where will I eat !? …

Trad.

There was a minimum of cinnamon in the
aluminum pan.

Anon.

<table>
<tr><td>**Video:** https://youtu.be/bRe-drzi1oI</td></tr>
<tr><td>**Audio:** https://audiomack.com/song/we_p/32-m</td></tr>
</table>

Video	Audio

Mary Mac

Mary Mac's mother's making Mary Mac marry
me. My mother's making me marry Mary
Mac. Will I always be so merry when Mary's
taking care of me? Will I always be so merry
when I marry Mary Mac?

Trad. (Scottish)

I see the moon, the moon sees me
God bless the man who baptised me.

Trad.

One man went to mow.

One man went to mow, went to mow a
meadow, one man and his dog, Spot, went to
mow a meadow. Two men went to mow,
went to mow a meadow, two men one man
and his dog, Spot, went to mow a meadow….

Anon.

Money and the Mare

"Lend me thy mare to ride a mile."
"She is lamed, leaping over a stile."
"Alack! and I must keep the fair!
I'll give thee money for thy mare."
"Oh, oh! say you so?
Money will make the mare to go!"

Trad.

Madam, I'm Adam.

Anon.

…The moan of doves in immemorial elms,
And murmuring of innumerable bees…

Tennyson

Common Words, Names and Phrases		
Monday	make	Mary
money	meet	Mohammed
morning	marry	Michael
Mummy	mad	Monica
May	moody	Melbourne
mean	remember	Mumbai
~to make ends meet~		
~there's a method to his madness~		
~the monkey in me made me do it~		
~a man must be his own master~		
~making a mountain out of a molehill~		

The Need of Needles

I need not your needles,
They're needless to me,
For the needing of needles
Is needless, you see.
But should my neat knickers
But need to be kneed,
I then should have need
Of your needles indeed.

Anon.

New York

You know New York. You need New York.
You know you need unique New York.

Anon.

Ninety nine nuns interred in an Indiana nunnery.

Anon.

A synonym for cinnamon is a cinnamon synonym.

Anon.

Many an anemone sees an enemy anemone.

Anon.

The Cannibal

How many cans can a cannibal nibble
if a cannibal can nibble cans?
A cannibal can nibble as many cans as a cannibal can nibble if a cannibal can nibble cans.

Anon.

There's no difference between Iranian uranium and Australian uranium.

SD Burke

Video: https://youtu.be/ceCyp7IynMo

Audio: https://audiomack.com/song/we_p/33-n

Nine nice night nurses nursing nicely.

Anon.

No, it's not the nun I know, it's another nun.

SD Burke

Now I know what I never knew I knew.

C Beasley.

Known Unknowns

As we know, there are known knowns; there are things we know we know. We also know there are known unknowns; that is to say we know there are some things we do not know. But there are also unknown unknowns—the ones we don't know we don't know.

D Rumsfeld

Giovanni has a noble, notable, knowing Roman nose.

SD Burke

Common Words, Names and Phrases		
name	need	Noah
night	notice	Nancy
nanny	nap	Penny
not	funny	Nigel
no	new	New York
end	in	Nigeria

~never say never~
~with friends like that who needs enemies?~
~a knight in shining armour~
~no news is good news~
~beware the enemy within~

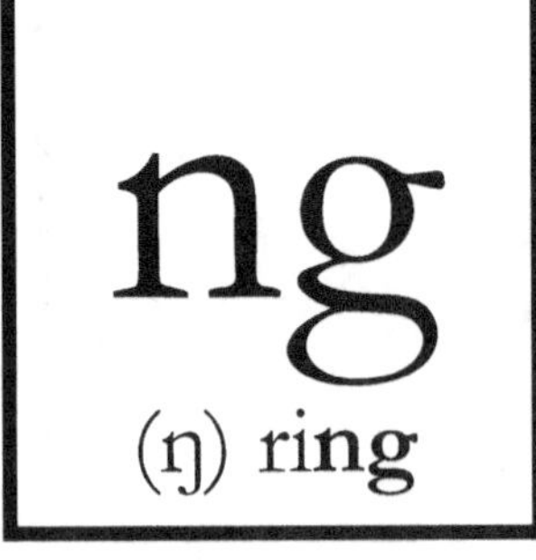

Person from Tring

A tone-deaf old person from Tring
When somebody asked him to sing
Replied, "It is odd
But I cannot tell "God
Save the Weasel" from "Pop goes the King".

Anon.

Sing a Song of Sixpence

Sing a song of sixpence, a pocket full of rye.
Four and twenty blackbirds baked in a pie.
When the pie was opened, the birds began to sing;
Wasn't that a dainty dish to set before the king?...

Trad.

Springtime

In the spring time, the only pretty ring time
Where birds do sing, hey ding a ding a ding
Sweet lovers love the spring.

Shakespeare

Bye Baby Bunting, daddy's gone a-hunting, to catch a little rabbit skin, to wrap his Baby Bunting in.

Trad.

Video: https://youtu.be/sKJvLtzkkm4	
Audio: https://audiomack.com/song/we_p/34-ng	
	Video	**Audio**

Come With Me

Come with me and dance with me, in the cool of autumn. All the trees are golden now, all the bells are ringing.
Ring, ring, ring, ring-a ding, ding dong, dance and sing together. Ring, ring, ring, ring-a ding, ding dong, in your shoes of leather.

Anon.

Are You Sleeping?

Are you sleeping? Are you sleeping?
Brother John, Brother John,
Morning bells are ringing! Morning bells are ringing! Ding Dang Dong. Ding Dang Dong

Trad (French)

from **The Walrus and the Carpenter**

"…The time has come," the Walrus said,
"To talk of many things:
Of shoes – and ships – and sealing wax
Of cabbages – and kings –
And why the sea is boiling hot –
And whether pigs have wings…"

L Carroll

Singing Along

As I was going along, long, long,
A singing a comical song, song, song,
The lane that I went was so long, long, long,
And the song that I sung was as long, long, long,
And so I went singing along.

Trad.

Common Words, Names and Phrases		
king	bring	Wang
song	ring	Ringo
long	angrily	Thingy
gang	wrong	Lang
singing	alarming	Singapore
belong	ingot	Hong Kong
~a bad beginning makes a bad ending~		
~hang on~		
~hang out~		
~bring it on~		
~sing for your supper~		

Yellow Bellied Sapsucker

You'll never guess, but yesterday, I saw one in
a tree. Yeah! In a tree, yesterday, at Yosemite,
You won't believe it, yesterday, a yard or so
from me. A yellow bellied sapsucker, just sitting in a tree!

SD Burke

You never count your money while you're
sitting at the table…

K Rogers

How many yaks could a yak pack pack if a yak
pack could pack yaks?

Anon.

Just Like You

Don't worry if your job is small,
And your rewards are few.
Remember that the mighty oak,
Was once a nut like you.

Anon.

Yoda

You're such a great Jedi Knight
Teaching others how to fight
You make them practise day and night
To defeat the Empire
They say that you're a workaholic
And though you're not a chocaholic
You may become an alcoholic
If you work on weekends
    Yoda, you gotta take it easy
    Yoda, try watching TV
    I know that you can fight and maim and
    kill. But Yoda, take a major chill pill.
    Try watching Kill Bill…

D Djurdjevic

Video: https://youtu.be/t1dz80lglVM	
Audio: https://audiomack.com/song/we_p/35-y	

The Lonely Goatherd

High on a hill was a lonely goatherd
lay hee, yodel ay ee, yodel ay hee hoo
Loud was the voice of the lonely goatherd
lay hee yodel ay hee yodal oh!

O Hammerstein II

The Tudor

A Tudor who tooted a flute
 tried to tutor two tooters to toot.
 Said the two to their tutor,
 "Is it harder to toot
 or to tutor two tooters to toot?"

C Wells

Young Lambs to Sell

If I'd as much money as I could tell,
I never would cry young lambs to sell;
Young lambs to sell, young lambs to sell;
I never would cry young lambs to sell.

Trad.

Common Words, Names and Phrases		
yesterday	yawn	Yasmin
year	use	Yolanda
you	young	Yogi
your	yes	Eunice
yell	cute	Yemen
yard	uniform	Cuba

~can't put an old head on young shoulders~
~youth is wasted on the young~
~he's a yes man~
~I wasn't born yesterday~
~your pride will be your undoing~

II

VOWEL SOUNDS

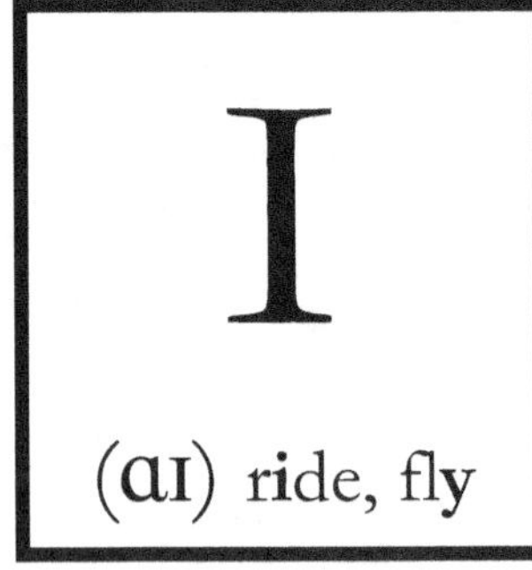

I
(ɑɪ) ride, fly

The Glutton
A glutton who came from the Rhine
Was asked at what hour he'd dine
He replied, "At eleven,
At three, five and seven,
And eight and a quarter to nine."

Anon.

The Young Lady of Riga
There was a young lady of Riga
Who smiled as she rode on a tiger
They returned from the ride
With the lady inside
And a smile on the face of the tiger

Anon.

There is a Lady
There is a lady sweet and kind,
Was never face so pleased my mind,
I did but see her passing by,
And yet I love her till I die…

Anon.

There was an old woman who swallowed a
fly.. I don't know why she swallowed a fly
….perhaps she'll die….

R Bonne

Video: https://youtu.be/dWYZrnjLylI

Audio: https://audiomack.com/song/we_p/38-ai

	Video	Audio

Three blind mice…

Trad.

The Charge of the Light Brigade
…Theirs not to make reply, theirs not to rea-
son why, theirs but to do and die…

Tennyson

Good night, sleep tight, don't let the bed bugs
bite.

Trad.

The Arrow
This morning when I woke I shot an arrow in
the sky. And as I stand here now, I know,
above me it does fly.
And just like yesterday, I know where it will
end its flight; upon the very bed where I will
smile and say goodnight.

SD Burke

Sir Belvidere
…Ah, my Lord Arthur, whither shall I go?
Where shall I hide my forehead and my eyes?
For now I see the true old times are dead…

Tennyson

Goodnight, Sweetheart, goodnight
The stars are shining bright,
The snow is turning white,
Dim is the failing light,
Fast falls the glooming night, —
   All right!   Sleep tight!   Goodnight.

M Twain

Common Words, Names and Phrases		
fly	ride	Michael
eye	cry	Brian
by	might	Caroline
buy	high	Ivan
my	wide	Brunei
night	lie	Iceland

~out of sight, out of mind~
~a stitch in time saves nine~
~red in the night, shepherd's delight~
~to see eye to eye~
~time flies~

The Queen of Hearts

The Queen of Hearts, she made some tarts,
All on a summer's day.
The Knave of Hearts, he stole the tarts,
And took them clean away.
The King of Hearts called for the tarts,
And beat the Knave full sore.
The Knave of Hearts brought back the tarts,
And vowed he'd steal no more.

Trad.

Not a Beauty

As a beauty I'm not a great star,
There are others more handsome by far,
But my face, I don't mind it,
Because I'm behind it--
'tis the folks in the front that I jar.

A Euwer

Car Park

How many cars would a car park park if a car
park could park cars?
A car park would park all it could park if a car
park could park cars.

E & P Tenni

Ask not what your country can do for you,
ask what you can do for your country.

JF Kennedy

Hark hark the dogs do bark

Hark hark the dogs do bark
The beggars are coming to town
Some in rags and some in jags
And one in a velvet gown.

Trad.

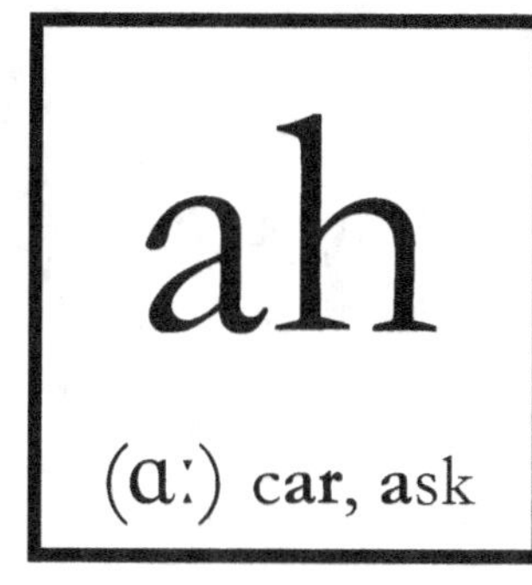

Swinging on a Star

Would you like to swing on a star?
Carry moonbeams home in a jar
And be better off than you are
Or would you rather be a mule?...

J Burke

Ah, the Moon!

But when words aren't enough to say
And A, eyes wide, just stands amazed
then all agree, both near and far
the only sound A makes is ah!
Ah, what beauty, Ah, what joy,
Remarkable Girl, Astonishing Boy
Ah! the sunset, Ah, that tune!
Alleluia! Ah, the moon!

SD Burke

Common Words, Names and Phrases		
bath	ask	Clara
are	harm	Carl
party	charge	Zara
car	hard	Arthur
banana	last	Kazakstan
laugh	large	Armenia

~part and parcel~
~a card shark~
~have a heart to heart~
~she's a hard task master~
~there's no harm in asking~

Video: https://youtu.be/hYc7lmHEU-c
Audio: https://audiomack.com/song/we_p/39-a

Video	Audio

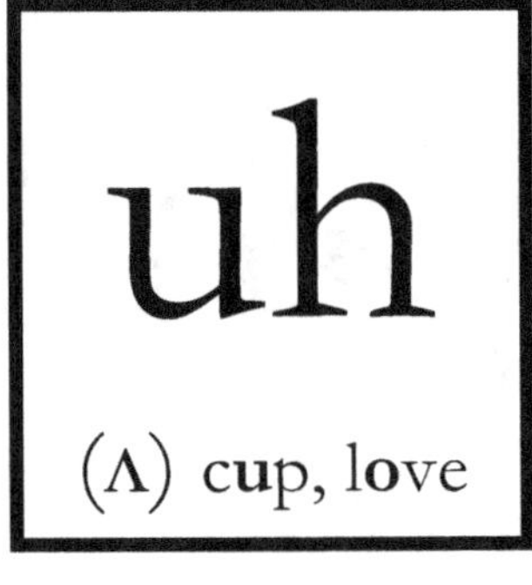

uh

(Λ) cup, love

Shut the Shutter

A mother to her son did utter
"Go, my son, and shut the shutter"
 "The shutter's shut" the son did utter
"I cannot shut it any shutter!"

Anon.

The Hippopotamus

…Mud, mud, glorious mud, there's nothing
quite like it for cooling the blood.
So follow me, follow, down to the hollow
And there let us wallow in glorious mud…

Flanders & Swann

I had a little nut tree

I had a little nut tree
Nothing would it bear
But a silver nutmeg and a golden pear
The king of Spain's daughter came to visit me
and all for the sake of my little nut tree

Trad.

A bucket of bug blood.

Anon.

Video: https://youtu.be/eDBZphY6zAI	
Audio: https://audiomack.com/song/we_p/40	

	Video	Audio

Unjust

The rain it raineth on the just and unjust fella,
but more upon the just because the unjust has
the just's umbrella.

C Bowen

Humpty Dumpty

Humpty Dumpty sat on a wall
Humpty Dumpty had a great fall
All the king's horses and all the king's men
Couldn't put Humpty together again.

Trad.

Double bubble gum bubbles double.

Anon.

Sippity Sup

Sippity sup, sippity sup
Bread and milk from a china cup
Bread and milk from a bright silver spoon
Made of a piece of the bright silver moon
Sippity sup, sippity sup
Sippity, sippity sup.

Trad.

Rub a dub dub

Rub a dub dub,
Three fools in a tub,
And who do you think they be?
The butcher, the baker,
The candlestick maker.
Turn them out, knaves all three.

Trad.

Common Words, Names and Phrases		
cup	study	Buddy
some	shut	Doug
duck	under	Rashima
nut	but	Honey
cut	Sunday	Busselton
become	love	Buffalo

~lucky in cards, unlucky in love~
~a month of Sundays~
~well begun is half done~
~what's done cannot be undone~
~he's just nuts~

Tinker, Tailor

Tinker, Tailor, Soldier, Sailor,
Rich Man, Poor Man, Beggar Man, Thief.

Trad.

Doctor Foster

Doctor Foster went to Gloucester,
In a shower of rain;
He stepped in a puddle,
Right up to his middle,
And never went there again.

Trad.

Mister!

She frowned and called him Mr.
Because he fondly kr.
And so for spite
That very night
That Mr. kr. sr.   *(Mist-ə kissed-ə sist-ə)*

Anon.

Little Polly Flinders

Little Polly Flinders sat among the cinders
Warming her pretty little toes
Her mother came and caught her
And whipped her little daughter
For spoiling her nice new clothes

Trad.

Brother from another mother.

Anon.

Lucy Locket

Lucy Locket lost her pocket,
Kitty Fisher found it
Not a penny was there in it
But a ribbon round it

Trad.

| Video: https://youtu.be/wFiyEzNIWak |
| Audio: https://audiomack.com/song/we_p/41 |

	Video	Audio

thə

(schwa)
rivER, todAY

The Tide in the River

The tide in the river, the tide in the river,
The tide in the river runs deep.
I saw a shiver pass over the river
As the tide turned in its sleep

E Farjeon

The Student Named Essar

There was once a student named Essar,
Whose knowledge got lesser and lesser.
It at last grew so small,
He knew nothing at all,
And now he's a college professor!

Anon.

Grey Goose and Grey Gander

Grey goose and grey gander
Waft your wings together
And carry the good king's daughter
Over the one-strand river

Trad.

Common Words, Names and Phrases		
mother	wonder	Anna
doctor	after	Alexander
letter	the	Hannah
summer	a	Tamara
answer	under	Canada
farmer	over	Kenya

~better late than never~
~nature is the best healer~
~here today, gone tomorrow~
~finders keepers, losers weepers~
~an apple a day keeps the doctor away~

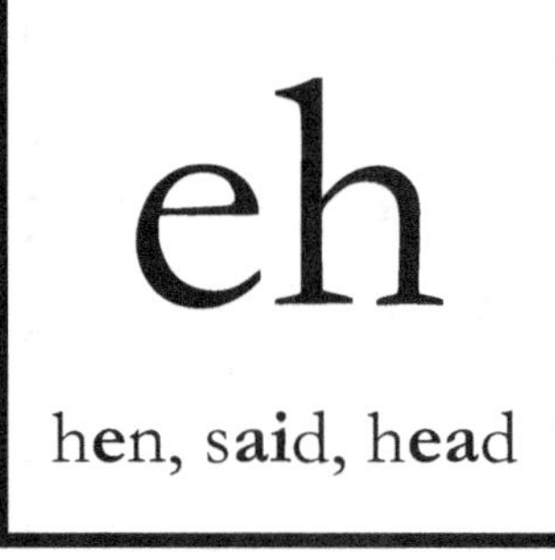

eh

hen, s**ai**d, h**ea**d

Teddy Bear

Teddy bear, teddy bear, turn around.
Teddy bear, teddy bear, touch the ground…

Anon.

My Black Hen

Hickety, pickety, my black hen,
She lays eggs for gentlemen;
Gentlemen come every day
To see what my black hen doth lay,
Sometimes nine and sometimes ten,
Hickety, pickety, my black hen.

Trad.

Five Little Monkeys

Five little monkeys jumping on the bed.
One fell off and bumped his head.
Mama called the doctor and the doctor said,
"No more monkeys jumping on the bed!..."

Anon.

Lesser leather never weathered wetter weather better.

Anon.

Eddie edited it.

Anon.

Video: https://youtu.be/0n6axnL4yhw
Audio: https://audiomack.com/song/we_p/42-e

	Video	Audio
Wonderful English		

Have You Ever?

Have you ever ever ever in your long legged life met a long legged sailor with a long legged wife?
No, I never never never in my long legged life met a long legged sailor with a long legged wife.

Anon.

Ella Ella Ate

Ella Ella ate eleven green peppers,
Eleven green peppers
from the green pepper tree.
Ella's gone green.
Get well, Ella.
Peck, peck, Ella green, green pepper tree.

SD Burke

Seventy seven benevolent elephants.

Anon.

Bandy Legs

As I was going to sell my eggs
I met a man with bandy legs,
Bandy legs and crooked toes;
I tripped up his heels, and he fell on his nose.

Trad.

The best breath test tests breath better.

Anon.

Common Words, Names and Phrases		
head	lend	Peggy
said	spend	Jessica
bed	get	Kenneth
leg	when	Teddy
red	then	Kenwick
any	bent	Denmark

~better late than never~
~Elvis has left the building~
~with friends like that, who needs enemies?~
~all's well that ends well~
~there's a remedy to everything but death~

Upon the Stair

Yesterday, upon the stair, I met a man who wasn't there.
He wasn't there again today; I wish, I wish, he would go away.

W Mearns

from The Arrow and the Song

I shot an arrow in the air
It fell to earth I know not where…

Longfellow

Leisure

What is this life if
Full of care
We have no time
To stand and stare?

WH Davies

There, They're and Their

They're in there, together, making all their plans.
They're in their little secret room, washing all their hands.
Their tongues are all on fire and their ears are burning, too.
They're plotting in their parlour, there, talking about you.

SD Burke

'Round the garden

'Round and 'round the garden
Like a teddy bear
One step, two step,
Tickle them under there

Trad.

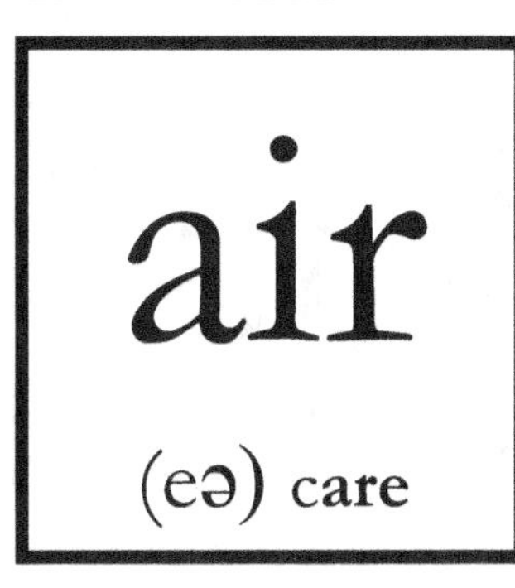

Pussy Cat, Pussy Cat

Pussy Cat, Pussy Cat, where have you been?
I've been to London to visit the queen.
Pussy Cat, Pussy Cat, what did you there?
I frightened a little mouse under her chair.

Trad.

from Lines and Squares

…I keep in the squares,
And the masses of bears,
Who wait at the corners all ready to eat
The sillies who tread on the lines of the street
Go back to their lairs,
And I say to them, "Bears,
Just look how I'm walking in all the squares!"..

AA Milne

Air hair lair

(what to say if you meet the queen)

Anon.

Where is Thumbkin? Where is Thumbkin?

Trad.

Common Words, Names and Phrases		
hair	care	Mary
chair	prepare	Bear
bear	dare	Arial
pair	fair	Eyre
where	bare	Cairns
heir	rare	Airmont

~fair's fair~
~share and share alike~
~there, there!~
~who dares, wins~
~the bare necessities~

Video: https://youtu.be/ogNoRAsG7ps
Audio: https://audiomack.com/song/we_p/43-e

	Video	Audio

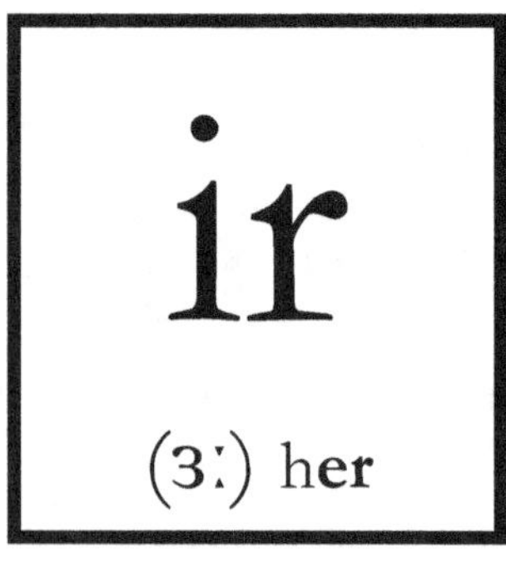

Mister!
She frowned and called him Mr.
Because he fondly kr.
And so for spite
That very night
That Mr. kr. sr.
(Mist 3: *kissed h* 3: *sist* 3:*)*

Anon.

Bernie Burke worked in Perth in a dirty shirt
to earn some burnt wurst

SD Burke

Mockingbird
Hush little baby don't say a word
 Mama's gonna buy you a mocking bird
If that mocking bird don't sing
Mama gonna buy you a diamond ring…

Trad.(USA)

Go to bed first
 Go to bed first, a golden purse ;
Go to bed second, a golden pheasant ;
Go to bed third, a golden bird !

Trad.

Video: https://youtu.be/LqVHd3dGHSc
Audio: https://audiomack.com/song/we_p/44-e

	Video	Audio

The Old Man of Vancouver
There was an old man of Vancouver
Whose wife got sucked in the hoover.
He said, "There's some doubt
If she's more in than out,
But whichever it is, I can't move her!"

Anon.

Wise Old Owl
A wise old owl lived in an oak
 The more he saw the less he spoke
The less he spoke the more he heard.
 Why can't we all be like that wise old bird?

Trad.(USA)

Larry Hurley, a burly squirrel hurler, hurled a
furry squirrel through a curly grill.

Anon.

Certified certificates from certified certificate
certifiers.

Anon.

Under the Earth
Under the earth, a dearth of light
A dearth of mirth, no need for sight
There the worm turns, in the endless night
Under the dark, dark earth.

SD Burke

Common Words, Names and Phrases		
bird	hurt	Fergie
girl	flirt	Bernard
word	curt	Ernest
work	stern	Vern
return	learn	Perth
her	turn	Berne

~first come, first served~
~the early bird catches the worm~
~a bird in the hand is worth
two in the bush~
~a can of worms~

The Young Girl of West Ham

There was a young girl of West Ham
Who hastily jumped on a tram.
When she had embarked
The conductor remarked,
"Your fare, Miss?" She answered, "I am."

Anon.

The Boy of Baghdad

There once was a boy of Baghdad,
An inquisitive sort of a lad,
Who said, "I will see
If a sting has a bee."
And he very soon found that it had!

Anon.

Ann and Andy's anniversary is in April.

Anon.

The Canner

A canner exceedingly canny
One morning remarked to his granny,
"A canner can can,
anything that he can
but a canner can't can a can, can he?"

C Wells

You cannae hand a man a grander spanner

Sidchrome ad. 1960s-

Jack Sprat

Jack Sprat could eat no fat.
His wife could eat no lean.
And so between them both, you see,
They licked the platter clean.

Trad.

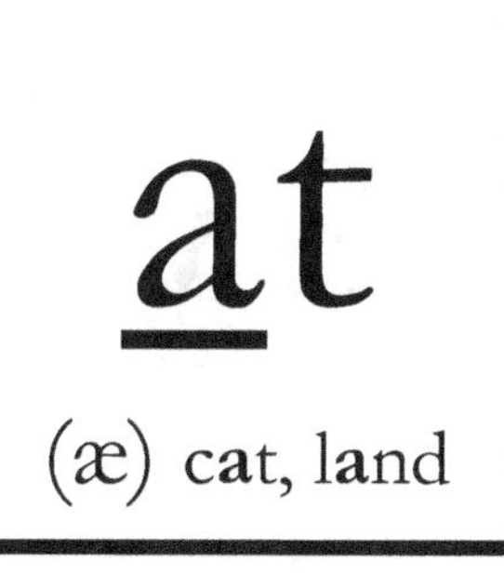

My Friend Gladys

Oh, the sadness of her sadness when she's
sad.
Oh, the gladness of her gladness when she's
glad.
But the sadness of her sadness,
and the gladness of her gladness,
Are nothing like her madness when she's mad!

Anon.

James, while John had had *"had"*, had had
"had had"; *"had had"* had had a better effect on
the teacher.

Anon.

Dan, Dan

Dan, Dan, the fine old man,
Washed his face in the frying pan,
Combed his hair with the leg of the chair,
Dan, Dan, the fine old man…

Trad.(Irish)

Common Words, Names and Phrases		
apple	ant	Ann
cat	bag	Anthony
at	have	Max
an	act	Madeline
am	stand	Angola
pants	and	Cambodia

~as mad as a hatter~
~let the cat out of the bag~
~a sprat to catch a mackerel~
~one of the lads~
~acting as the bag man~

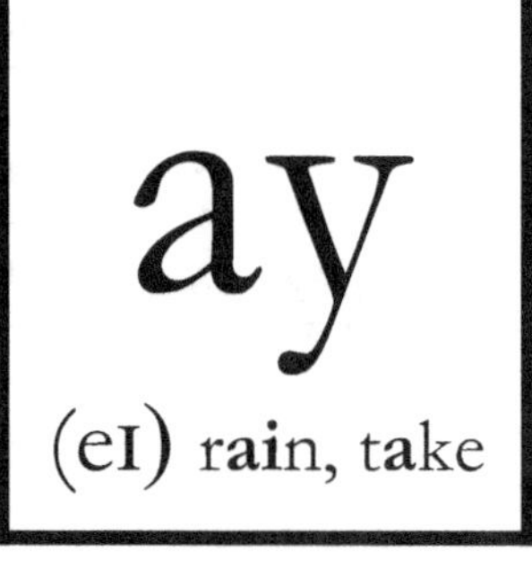

ay

(eɪ) rain, take

Painful James

James, James went to great pains
To find different ways to behave.
He said, "I'm a failure if even one day
goes by when I act just the same."
James, James, James drove his teachers insane
With tortuous labours and mischievous
games.
They all just went crazy -and some became
lame- due to the persistent rain that was
James.

SD Burke

Pat a Cake

Pat a cake pat a cake baker's man,
Bake me a cake as fast as you can…

Trad.

What Tate Ate

I know a boy named Tate who dined with his
girl at eight eight. I'm unable to state what
Tate ate at eight eight or what Tate's tête à
tête ate at eight eight.

Anon.

Video: https://youtu.be/iF9zl8g-Sys
Audio: https://audiomack.com/song/we_p/46-ei

	Video	Audio

Fedelma's Song

Oh good king's son, it must be done
Just the way I say
Take out your sword, no further word
And take my life away
Collect each bone, and drive it home
To make the dark stairway
Descend the stair, find the ring there
And carry it away
Ascend in haste, each bone in place
And make me whole again.

SD Burke

The rain in Spain stays mainly in the plain

G Pascal

The Teacher

I'd like to be a teacher, and have a clever
brain, calling out, "Attention, please!" and
"Must I speak in vain?"
I'd be quite strict with boys and girls whose
minds I had to train, and all the books and
maps and things I'd carefully explain;
I'd make then learn the dates of kings, and all
the capes of Spain;
   But I wouldn't be a teacher if …   I couldn't
use the cane.   Would you?

CJ Dennis

Rain, rain, go away, come again another day.

Trad.

Common Words, Names and Phrases		
baby	stay	Jason
rain	day	Freya
take	grey	Caitlin
away	may	Ray
mate	stray	Spain
wait	aim	Jamaica
~an apple a day keeps the doctor away~		
~fortune favours the brave~		
~on the same page~		
~no pain, no gain~		
~fake it 'til you make it~		

from **The Walrus and the Oysters**

"A loaf of bread," the Walrus said, "Is what
we chiefly need: Pepper and vinegar besides
 Are very good indeed- Now if you're ready,
Oysters dear, We can begin to feed."

L Carroll

Phoebe Beebee

A certain young fellow named Beebee
Wished to marry a lady named Phoebe
"But," he said. "I must see
What the minister's fee be
Before Phoebe be Phoebe Beebee"

Anon.

I scream, you scream, we all scream for
icecream

Johnson, Moll & King

The Duchess

I sat next to the Duchess at tea; It was just as
I feared it would be. Her rumblings ab-
dominal Were simply phenomenal,
And everyone thought it was me!

Anon.

I before e, except after c, whenever the word
rhymes with me.

Trad.

Andy Pandy, sugar and candy, all jump up.
Andy Pandy, sugar and candy, all jump down.

Trad.

Here is the church, here is the steeple
Look inside and here are the people.

Trad.

Kookaburra sits in the old gum tree
Merry merry king of the bush is he…

M Sinclair

Video: https://youtu.be/UisCQtU2528	
Audio: https://audiomack.com/song/we_p/47-i	
	Video	Audio

ee

(iː) **ea**t, sk**i**

From the Earth

From the earth comes the tree
Branches stretch wide as can be
Falling, falling, little leaves
Down to earth, little leaves
From the earth comes the tree.

SD Burke

The Forest Stands

The forest stands alone in me
A million trees from sea to sea
I hunt beneath the canopy
For every flower and every bee
The forest stands alone in me.

SD Burke

One, two, three, I love coffee and Billy loves
tea. How good you be! One, two, three,
I love coffee and Billy loves tea.

Trad.

Read my riddle, I pray: What God never sees,
the king seldom sees and we see every day.

Anon.

Common Words, Names and Phrases		
feet	bee	Evie
thirteen	read	Peter
tree	keep	Jean
believe	free	Yvonne
eat	greedy	Tahiti
leave	compete	Hungary
~a friend in need is a friend indeed~		
~seeing is believing~		
~freedom and responsibility~		
~she's the bee's knees~		
~my heart bleeds~		

i

sit, in, pin

The Mathematician of Trinity

A mathematician of Trinity
Was computing the cube of infinity
But the number of digits soon gave him such
fidgets he dropped it and took up divinity

G Gamow

Pretty Kitty

Pretty Kitty, witty Kitty. Pretty witty little Kitty sitting in the middle of a little tin house.
Neat as a pin and clean as a whistle, skinny
and silly and timid as a mouse.
Pretty Kitty, fickle Kitty, pretty witty little Kitty. Pretty, witty, skinny, silly, fickle, timid little
Kitty sitting in the middle of a little tin house.

SD Burke

Bitter Biting Bittern

A bitter biting bittern bit a better biting bittern, and the better biting bittern bit him
back. Said the bitter biting bittern to the better biting bittern
"I'm a bitter biting bittern bitten back"

Anon.

Six little mice sat down to spin…

Trad.

Video: https://youtu.be/WToVmnpdlu8
Audio: https://audiomack.com/song/we_p/48-i

	Video	Audio

The Young Lady of Lynn

There was a young lady of Lynn
Who was so uncommonly thin
That when she essayed to drink lemonade
She slipped through the straw and fell in

Anon.

The fishwife stood on the silver balcony, in-explicably mimicking him hiccuping, and
amicably welcoming him in.

Anon.

Michael Finnigan

There once was a man named Michael Finne-gan, he grew whiskers on his chinnegan,
The wind came up and blew them innegan
Poor old Michael Finnegan (begin again)…

Trad. (Irish)

My Paddle's Clean and Bright

Dip, dip and swing her back, flashing with
silver, follow the wild goose track, dip, dip
and swing…

ME McGee

Fish and chips and vinegar, vinegar, vinegar.
Fish and chips and vinegar, pepper, pepper,
pepper, salt.

Anon.

There's many a slip 'twixt cup and lip.

Trad.

Common Words, Names and Phrases		
tin	it	Kim
ship	in	Isabelle
fit	big	Mick
sit	inside	India
pick	into	Italy
win	hit	Mississippi

~from little things big things grow~
~add insult to injury~
~he will flip his lid~
~a dish fit for a king~
~loose lips sink ships~
~put lipstick on a pig~

The Young Fellow Named Weir

There was a young fellow named Weir
Who hadn't an atom of fear;
He indulged a desire
To touch a live wire
'Most any last line will do here.

Anon.

Baby Dear

Where did you come from, Baby Dear?
Out of the everywhere into the here
Where did you get those eyes so blue?
Out of the sky as I came through
What makes the light in them sparkle and spin?
Some of the starry spikes left in
Where did you get that little tear?
I found it waiting when I got here…

G MacDonald

He who has ears to hear, let him hear

Gospels

All the world is queer save thee and me, and even thou art a little queer.

R Owen

The only thing we have to fear is fear itself.

FD Roosevelt

The Old Man with a Beard

There was an Old Man with a beard,
Who said, "It is just as I feared!—
Two Owls and a Hen, four Larks and a Wren,
Have all built their nests in my beard."

E Lear

Near an ear, a nearer ear, a nearly eerie ear.

Anon.

Video: https://youtu.be/D54-cM2DIRo
Audio: https://audiomack.com/song/we_p/49-i

	Video	Audio

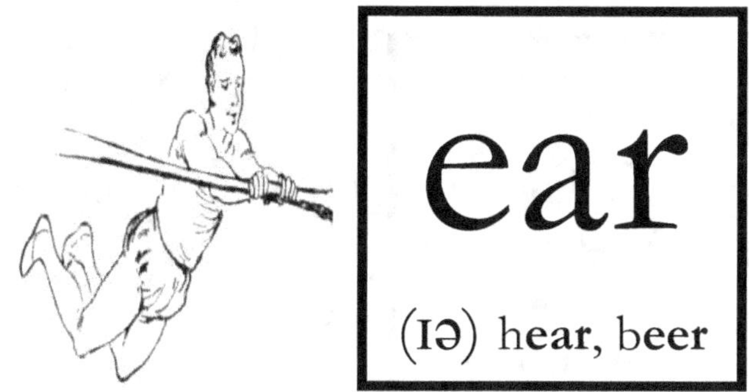

The Rainy Day

The day is cold, and dark, and dreary;
It rains, and the wind is never weary;
The vine still clings to the mouldering wall,
But at every gust the dead leaves fall,
And the day is dark and dreary…

Longfellow

Lydia

Lydia, oh! Lydia, say have you met Lydia?
Oh! Lydia, the tattooed lady.
She has eyes that folks adore so
And a torso even more so
Lydia, oh! Lydia, that "Encyclopedia,"
Oh! Lydia, the Queen of tattoo…

Y Harburg & H Arlen

…God bless our noble parliament,
And rid them from all fears !
God bless all th' *commons* of this land,
And God bless *some* o' th' peers !

Trad.

Common Words, Names and Phrases		
ear	appear	Leah
beer	dreary	Guinevere
pier	sheer	Belvedere
experience	here	Mia
weary	hear	Noumea
deal	near	Tanzania
~I'm all ears~		
~play it by ear~		
~here today, gone tomorrow~		
~hear, hear!~		
~life's not all beer and skittles~		

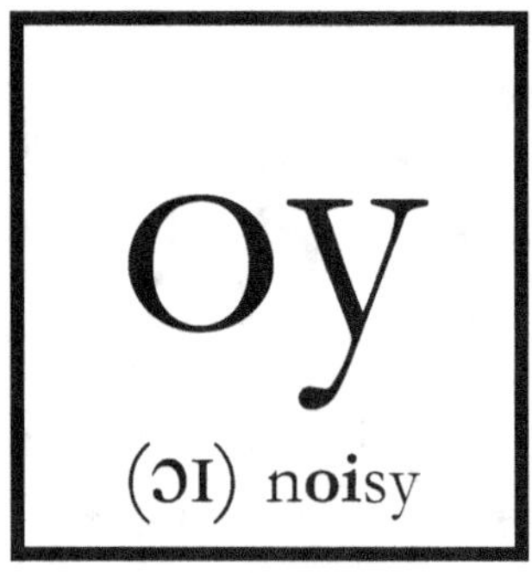

oy
(ɔɪ) no**i**sy

Any noise annoys an oyster but a noisy noise annoys an oyster most.

Anon.

Loyal Roy
Roy was a boy most loyal to the royals,
He found his greatest joy in royal employ.
His loyalty could be neither spoiled nor foiled,
A simply most joyful royal-loyal boy, Roy.

SD Burke

What are Little Boys Made of?
What are little boys made of?
What are little boys made of?
Frogs and snails and puppy dogs tails
That's what little boys are made of…

Trad.

Hey, Ho
When that I was and a little tiny boy,
With hey, ho, the wind and the rain,
A foolish thing was but a toy,
For the rain it raineth every day…

Shakespeare

Old, oily Ollie oils old, oily autos.

Anon.

Video: https://youtu.be/Ng3pnp3qMGc
Audio: https://audiomack.com/song/we_p/50-oi

	Video	Audio

How much oil can a gum boil boil if a gum boil can boil oil?

Anon.

Joy to the World
…Joy to the world, the Savior reigns. Let men their songs employ. While fields and floods
Rocks, hills and plains
Repeat the sounding joy, repeat the sounding joy, repeat, repeat, the sounding joy…

I Watts

The Wild Colonial Boy
There was a wild colonial boy, Jack Doolan was his name. Of poor but honest parents he was born in Castlemaine.
He was his father's only son, his mother's pride and joy, and dearly did his parents love the wild colonial boy

Trad.

Enjoy.
Millions of years. A world enjoyed.
But then, abruptly, out of the void. An Asteroid. All destroyed.
Millions of years….A world enjoyed…

SD Burke

Oyster Stew
An oyster met an oyster, and they were oysters two; Two oysters met two oysters, And they were oysters too; Four oysters met a pint of milk, And they were oyster stew.

Anon.

Common Words, Names and Phrases		
boy	destroy	Joy
soil	coy	Troy
toy	oily	Lloyd
boil	spoilt	Malfoy
enjoy	avoid	Oyster Bay
alkaloid	point	Poynton
~burn the midnight oil~		
~oil the wheels~		
~boys will be boys~		
~a watched pot never boils~		
~boys' toys~		

I Saw Esau

I saw Esau kissing Kate, Kate saw I saw Esau
Esau saw that I saw Kate, and Kate saw I saw
Esau. I saw Esau kissing Kate -- the fact is,
we all three saw. For I saw her, and she saw
me, And she saw I saw Esau.

Anon.

War No More

Gonna lay down my sword and shield
Down by the riverside, down by the riverside,
down by the riverside
Gonna lay down my sword and shield
Down by the riverside,
Gonna study war no more
    I ain't gonna study war no more…

Trad (USA)

from The Windhover

I caught this morning, morning's minion.
Kingdom of daylight's dauphin. Dapple
dawn-drawn falcon. In his riding…

GM Hopkins

Knife and a fork, bottle and a cork
that is the way you spell New York.

Anon.

How many boards could the Mongols hoard if
the Mongol hordes got bored?

B Waterson

A cat has claws on the ends of its paws.
A comma's a pause at the end of a clause.

Anon.

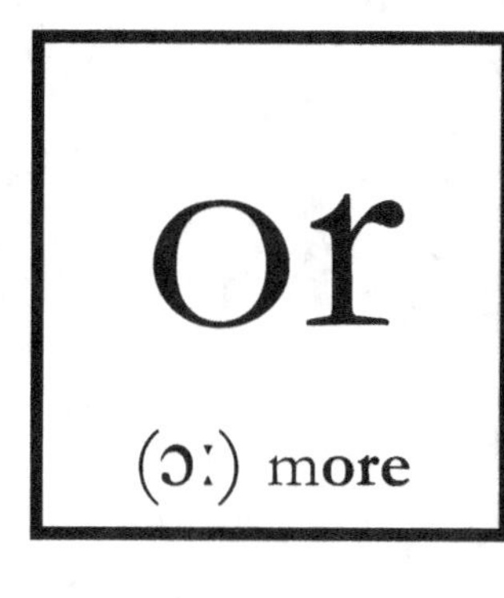

It's Raining, It's Pouring

It's raining, it's pouring.
The old man is snoring.
He went to bed and bumped his head,
And couldn't get up in the morning.

Trad.

The Man of Bengal

There once was a man of Bengal
Who was asked to a fancy-dress ball;
He said, "I will risk it
And go as a biscuit"
But a dog ate him up in the hall.

Anon.

Humpty Dumpty

Humpty Dumpty sat on a wall
Humpty Dumpty had a great fall
Three score men and three score more,
Cannot place Humpty Dumpty as he was before.

Trad.

Video: https://youtu.be/JYSUzJS5SWg
Audio: https://audiomack.com/song/we_p/51-o

	Video	Audio

Common Words, Names and Phrases		
corn	caught	Laura
shawl	door	Maureen
call	awful	Maude
horse	ordinary	Audrey
fall	awkward	Jordan
talk	sort	Orlando

~red in the morning, shepherd's warning~
~the ball is in your court~
~horses for courses~
~lead a horse to water~
~pride comes before a fall~

OW

(aʊ) house

The Lion and the Unicorn
The lion and the unicorn were fighting for the crown
The lion beat the unicorn all around the town.
Some gave them white bread, and some gave them brown;
Some gave them plum cake and drummed them out of town.

Trad.

I'm a Little Teapot
I'm a little teapot, short and stout
Here is my handle, here is my spout
When I get all steamed up, hear me shout
Tip me over, pour me out!

Trad.

from **Our House**
Our house it has a crowd
There's always something happening
And it's usually quite loud
Our mum she's so house-proud
Nothing ever slows her down
And a mess is not allowed
Our house, in the middle of our street
Our house, in the middle of our…

C Foreman & C Smyth

| Video: https://youtu.be/lAqKt-sFDnc |
| Audio: https://audiomack.com/song/we_p/52-au |

	Video	Audio

How now brown cow?

Anon.

Frown Down
If we're happy then we smile
But when we're angry, then we frown
For a smile the mouth goes up
And for a frown the mouth goes down

SD Burke

'Twas the night before Christmas, when all through the house, not a creature was stirring, not even a mouse…

CC Moore

Little Mousey Brown
Up the tall white candlestick
Climbed little mousey brown
Right to the top, but he couldn't get down
So he called to his grandma
"Grandma, grandma"
But grandma was in town
So he curled himself into a ball
What a clever mouse!
And rolled himself back down.

Trad.

Be a Clown
Be a clown, be a clown
All the world loves a clown…
Be a clown, be a clown, be a clown

C Porter

Common Words, Names and Phrases		
cow	bow	Howard
about	frown	Mao
down	allow	Rowley
around	now	Ploughman
eyebrow	house	Macau
plough		Georgetown

~when in doubt. leave it out~
~get out of town~
~he's down at the mouth~
~stop clowning around~
~as quiet as a mouse~

Proper Cup of Coffee

What I want is a proper cup of coffee made in a proper cup of coffee pot. I may be off my dot but I do want a proper cup of coffee made in a proper cup of coffee pot. Tin coffee pots and iron coffee pots, they're no use to me. If I can't have a proper cup of coffee made in a proper cup of coffee pot, I'll have a cup of tea.

R Weston & W Lee

Lock Up Your Stock

If you stick a stock of liquor in your locker,
It's slick to stick a lock upon your stock,
Or some stickler who is slicker
Will stick you of your liquor
If you fail to lock your liquor
With a lock!

Anon.

Jolly Phonics!

Chris Jolly

Hot cross buns, hot cross buns, one a penny, two a penny, hot cross buns…

Trad.

Dull Dark Dock

To sit in solemn silence in a dull, dark dock,
In a pestilential prison, with a life-long lock…

Gilbert & Sullivan

Chop shops stock chops.

Anon.

| Video: https://youtu.be/BOuS0wxh0h8 |
| Audio: https://audiomack.com/song/we_p/53-a |

| | Video | Audio |

(ɒ) pot, often

God in the Quad

There once was a man who said, "God,
Must think it exceedingly odd
If he finds that this tree
Continues to be
When there's no one about in the Quad."

R Knox

Dear Sir, your astonishment's odd
I am always about in the Quad
And that's why this tree
continues to be
Since observed by, Yours faithfully, God.

Fr. Valentine

Pease Porridge Hot

Pease porridge hot, pease porridge cold,
Pease porridge in the pot, nine days old.
Some like it hot, some like it cold,
Some like it in the pot, nine days old.

Trad

Common Words, Names and Phrases		
octopus	got	Holly
office	hot	Johnny
robin	on	Oliver
copy	opposite	Wally
offer	onto	Oxford
odd	off	Solomons

~honesty is the best policy~
~he's off his rocker~
~going off like a frog in a sock~
~knock your socks off~
~a watched pot never boils~
~when sorrow is asleep, wake it not~

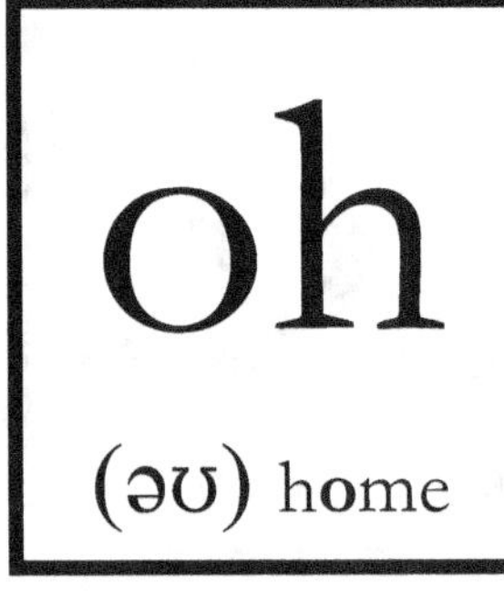

oh

(əʊ) home

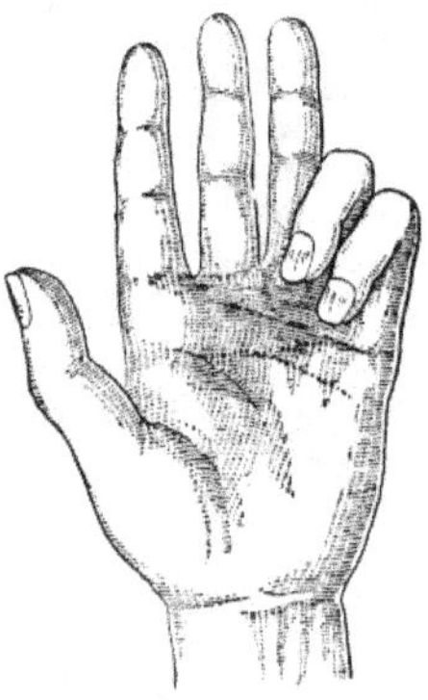

Row Row Row Your Boat
Row row row your boat, gently down the stream
Merrily, merrily, merrily, merrily, life is but a dream.

Anon.

To Morrow
A traveler once to his sorrow
Requested a ticket to Morrow.
Said the railman, "It's plain
That there isn't a train
To Morrow today, but tomorrow."

Anon.

Old King Cole
Old King Cole was a merry old soul
And a merry old soul was he;
He called for his pipe, and he called for his bowl. And he called for his fiddlers three.

Trad.

There Were Five in the Bed
There were five in the bed and the little one said, "Roll over, roll over,"
So they all rolled over and one fell out…

Trad.

Video: https://youtu.be/6dhlbJgevjw	
Audio: https://audiomack.com/song/we_p/54-u	

Video	Audio

Moses Supposes
Moses supposes his toeses are roses,
  But Moses supposes erroneously,
  For nobody's toeses are posies of roses,
  As Moses supposes his toeses to be.

B Comden & A Green

Fingers and Toes
I'd rather have fingers than toes;
I'd rather have ears than a nose;
And as for my hair
I'm glad it's all there,
  I'll be awfully sad when it goes.

G Burges

Ring-a-Rosies
Ring a ring a rosies, a pocket full of posies
a-tissue, a-tissue, we all fall down.

Trad.

Oats, peas, beans
Oats, peas, beans and barley grow
Oats, peas, beans and barley grow
Do you or I or anyone know
How oats, peas, beans and barley grow?

Trad.

The Groat
There was an old man in a velvet coat,
He kiss'd a maid and gave her a groat ;
The groat was crack'd, and would not go,—
Ah, old man, d'ye serve me so ?

Trad.

Common Words, Names and Phrases		
coat	so	Willow
toe	know	Joseph
boat	only	Bruno
home	window	Obie
hope	own	Oklahoma
open	low	Cambodia

~he knows the ropes~
~rolling in dough~
~in the same boat~
~toe the line~
~home sweet home~

Two and Two

There was a young man who said, "Do
Tell me how I'm to add two and two.
I'm not very sure
That it doesn't make four -
But I fear that it's almost too few."

Anon.

The Old Man of Peru

There was an old man of Peru
Who dreamt he was eating his shoe
He woke in the night
In a terrible fright
And found it was perfectly true.

Anon.

The Old Man of Dunoon

There was an old man of Dunoon
Who ate soup with a very small spoon.
For he said, "As I eat
Neither fish, fowl, nor meat,
I should otherwise finish too soon."

Anon.

The New Gnu

One day I went to the zoo
For I wanted to see the old gnu;
But the old gnu was dead
And the new gnu they said
Was too new a new gnu to view.

Anon.

How do you do? How do you do?
Just like a laddu, one pais: two.

Trad. (India)

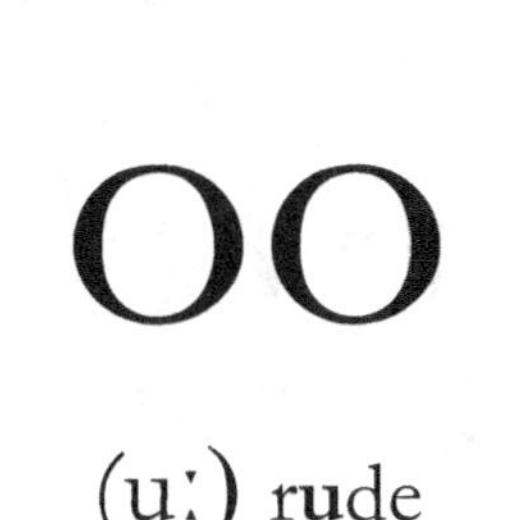

The Tudor

A Tudor who tooted a flute
 tried to tutor two tooters to toot.
Said the two to their tutor,
"Is it harder to toot
 or to tutor two tooters to toot?"

C Wells

Ah Choo

Old Man, Ah Choo,
Master of Kung Fu.
Bows low, Smiles at you,
Suddenly, you're black and blue.
Lesson over.
Thank you,
Ah Choo.
Bless you,
Ah Choo,
Bless you.

S Burke

Common Words, Names and Phrases		
moon	to	Julia
spoon	too	Ruth
balloon	two	Luke
move	blue	Trudy
prove	true	Vanuatu
suit	through	Tuvalu

~the moon is made of blue cheese~
~once in a blue moon~
~do unto others~
~beauty is truth, truth, beauty~
~an eye for an eye, a tooth for a tooth~

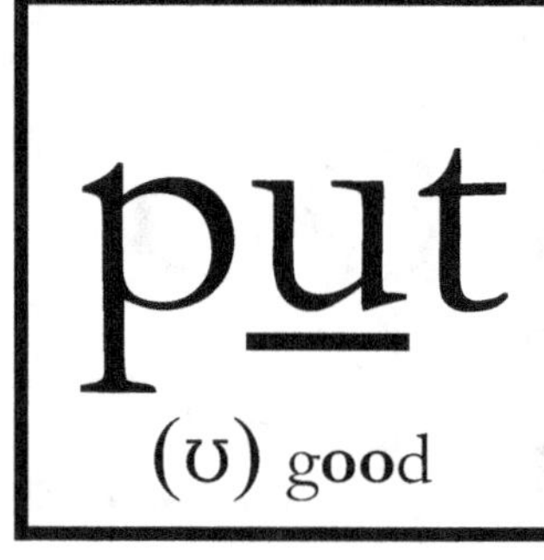

Chook Book

How many books would a good chook book
if a good chook could book books?
A good chook would book all he could book
 if a good chook could book books.
(buk! buk!)

SD Burke

How many cookies could a good cook cook if
a good cook could cook cookies?

Anon.

From **Wooden Heart**

…Treat me nice,
treat me good,
treat me like you really should
'cause I'm not made of wood
and I don't have a wooden heart…

F Wise &ors

Good Morning

Good morning, good morning
We've danced the whole night through
Good morning, good morning to you…

A Freed

| Video: https://youtu.be/pvPWT8AGlro |
| Audio: https://audiomack.com/song/we_p/56-u |

	Video	Audio

Three Little Birds

There were three little birds in a wood
Who always sang hymns when they could.
What the words were about
You could never make out,
But you felt it was doing them good.

Anon.

There Was a Crooked Man

There was a crooked man
Who walked a crooked mile
He found a crooked sixpence
Upon a crooked stile
He bought a crooked cat
Which caught a crooked mouse
And they all lived together in a little crooked
house.

Trad.

From **We Wish You a Merry Christmas**

Now bring us some figgy pudding,
Now bring us some figgy pudding,
Now bring us some figgy pudding,
And bring some out here.
Good tidings I bring
To you and your kin;
I wish you a merry Christmas
And a happy New Year.

Trad.

By hook or by crook, I'll be first in the book.

Trad.

Common Words, Names and Phrases		
foot	put	Brooke
book	good-bye	Rahule
could	would	Tulsi
would	pudding	Cook
hook	cook	Tobruk
took	pull	Burundi

~Pull the wool over his eyes~
~to play hookey~
~in her good books~
~put your best foot forward~
~cooking the books~

Tour of the Moor

Up in Yorkshire one may cycle on a tour of
the moor, whilst in Brighton there's the op-
tion of a tour of the sewer.
One is thus put to the challenge of which tour
to procure
But contrasting the gay clatter and the cyclists'
happy chatter , with the dark and danky odour
of the cavern of the ratter
One is highly recommended to ensure against
the latter.

SD Burke

The Curate

I remember the time that our Curate
Caught a cold and he wanted to cure it
But the pills that he tried
Made him sick, and he died
He'd have been better off to endure it.

Anon.

The Brewer Tour

We were starting to think it was rash
To have paid our deposit in cash
For

Terence J Brewer's
European Tour
Self-proclaimed epicure
Continental connoisseur
Expert on the quirky and obscure

Yes,
we were allured, but only to find
The same Terence J Brewer
Was also a kind
of expert in the hundred yard dash.

SD Burke

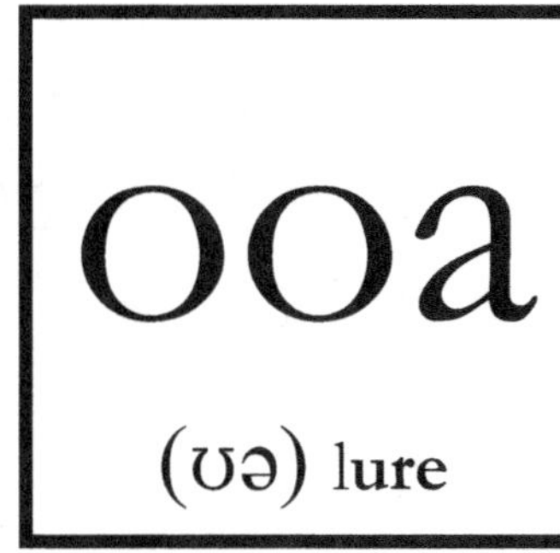

The Maiden of Glenmalure

A coy maiden of Glenmalure,
Had a mind that was perfectly pure.
She fainted away,
In a delicate way,
If anyone spoke of manure.

Anon.

Louis Pasteur

The hero of every home brewer,
Is a Frenchman that's known as Pasteur.
His knowledge of bugs
Has improved many mugs
Of old ale, with the taste of a sewer.

Anon.

Video: https://youtu.be/BHR-0oQKwI4		
Audio: https://audiomack.com/song/we_p/57-u		
	Video	Audio

Common Words, Names and Phrases		
tour	ensure	Brewer
sewer	procure	Jewel
moor	immature	Azure
endure	demure	Purest
lure	manure	Nuku'alofa
cure	masseur	Tours
~get out of the sewer~		
~beware the moor~		
~the cure is worse than the disease~		
~as pure as driven snow~		
~pure cures are fewer and fewer~		

III

CONSONANT BLENDS

Gobbling gargoyles gobbled gobbling goblins.

Anon.

Blair's all black bike was better than Blane's all blue bike and much better than Brody's blue and black bike.

SD Burke

Blue Girl Beer
Blue Girl Beer is a beautiful brew
It's the best beer from Bremen and Hong Kong too. Bring a big, big bottle of the blue girl brew 'cos banging back a bluey is how my love for the blue girl grew!

SD Burke

Big black bugs bleed blue blood but big blue bugs bleed black blood.

Anon.

Whereat with blade, with bloody, blameful blade, he bravely broached his boiling bloody breast.

Shakespeare

…Blow, blow, blow 'til I be but breath of the spirit, blowing in me…

MT Winter

| Video: https://youtu.be/H7Y_7c_H3Rg |
| Audio: https://audiomack.com/song/we_p/60-bl |

	Video	Audio

Cobbler, cobbler, Mend my shoe,
Get it done by half past two..

Trad.

Bless the Earth
Bless the earth that I stand on
Bless each fruit and grain therefrom
Bless the hands that help me grow
Bless the centre of my home
Bless the source of rivers deep
Living water in my sleep
Bless each sound that I create
Bless each thought that flies to fate
Bless each one, each friend I see
King of heaven, blessed be.

SD Burke

Bunch of blue ribbons
Oh, dear, what can the matter be?
Johnny's so long at the fair.
He promised he'd buy me a bunch of blue ribbons. He promised he'd buy me a bunch of blue ribbons. He promised he'd buy me a bunch of blue ribbons to tie up my bonny brown hair.

Trad.

Blow the Man Down
Come all ye young fellows that follows the sea
To me, way hey, blow the man down
Now please pay attention and listen to me
Give me some time to blow the man down…

Trad.

Common Words, Names and Phrases		
blood	blow	Blossom
blunder	block	Blair
bloke	blue	Blane
blubber	black	Blaise
bleed	bloody	Blackburn
blind	blond	Blacktown
~as blind as a bat~ ~a blessing in disguise~ ~feeling blue~ ~the blind leading the blind~ ~my heart bleeds for you~		

Brilliant Boring Brian

Brian Brady was a bright boy and so it's
strange but true
That Brian found himself boring, and others
thought so too
"Brian Brady's boring!" the other boys would
say
And Brian agreed and also wished that he
could run away
But then one day it happened; Brian had a
bright idea
And all the boys from near and far flocked
from far and near.
"Brian Brady's brilliant!" all the boys did say
But Brian found them boring, and wished
they'd go away.

SD Burke

Celibate celebrant, celibate celebrant, celibate
celebrant.

Anon.

My Bonnie lies over the ocean

My Bonnie lies over the ocean
My Bonnie lies over the sea
My Bonnie lies over the ocean
So bring back my Bonnie to me
Bring back, oh, bring back
Bring back my Bonnie to me, to me
Bring back, oh, bring back
Bring back my Bonnie to me.

Trad.

The British bloke's back brake block broke.

Anon.

Bake big batches of bitter brown bread.

Anon.

Bryan O'Lin

Bryan O'Lin, and his wife, and wife's mother,
They all went over a bridge together :
The bridge was broken, and they all fell in,
The deuce go with all ! quoth Bryan O'Lin.

Trad.

Brown Bread

You still may make white bread and cake,
By style and fancy led,
But I tell you, sir, that I prefer
A loaf of good brown bread.

NE Farmer.

| Video: https://youtu.be/OTidVGE37LA |
| Audio: https://audiomack.com/song/we_p/61-br |

Video	Audio

Common Words, Names and Phrases		
brother	bring	Brian
bread	breathe	Brenda
broom	brief	Bradley
break	bright	Brown
brawn	brave	Brunei
brazen	abrupt	Brazil

~bring home the bacon~
~he's more brawn than brains~
~as bold as brass~
~break a leg~
~make a clean breast of it~

The Train
Clickety, Clickety, Clack.
Clickety, Clickety, Clack.
Clickety, Clickety, Clickety, Clickety,
Clickety, Clickety, Clack.
Here comes the old train along the rickety track.

Trad.

Click go the Shears
Click go the shears, boys, click, click, click.
Wide is his blow and his hands move quick,
The ringer looks around and he's beaten by a blow
And he curses that old snagger with the blue-bellied yoe.

Trad.(Aust.)

-Stand clear of the closing doors, please!
(New York Subway)

C Pellett

Hickory dickory dock, the mouse ran up the clock, the clock struck one, the mouse ran down, hickory dickory dock.

Trad.

Video: https://youtu.be/6ldDYtVxJNs	
Audio: https://audiomack.com/song/we_p/62-cl	

Video	Audio

Clap Your Hands
If you're happy and you know it, clap your hands.
If you're happy and you know it, clap your hands.
If you're happy and you know it, then you really ought to show it
If you're happy and you know it, clap your hands ....

Anon.

Horsie, Horsie
Horsie horsie don't you stop
Just let your feet go clippity clop
Your tail go swish and the wheels go 'round
Giddy-up, we're homeward bound.

Trad.

A clean clam crammed in a clean clam can.
Clean clams crammed in clean clam cans.

Anon.

The Clock
There's a neat little clock,
In the schoolroom it stands,
And it points to the time
With its two little hands.
And may we, like the clock,
Keep a face clean and bright,
With hands ever ready
To do what is right.

Trad.

Common Words, Names and Phrases		
class	climb	Claudia
cloud	clever	Clarence
clown	clear	Clara
clap	clumsy	Clarissa
clean	close	Clare
acclimatise	decline	Cleveland

~as clear as mud~
~a close call~
~to clip their wings~
~clear the air~
~make a clean breast of it~

Connor McCracken

Connor McCracken was a cracking fine lad
He crushed all his enemies dead
A little bit crazy, perhaps, but that said,
There was never a critical word to be heard
For his crisp execution with mace, axe or sword,
or the way that he cracked you right over the head.

SD Burke

From **Birches**

They click upon themselves
As the breeze rises, and turn many-colored
As the stir cracks and crazes their enamel.
Soon the sun's warmth makes them shed crystal shells
Shattering and avalanching on the snow-crust—

R Frost

There Was a Crooked Man

There was a crooked man, who walked a crooked mile. He found a crooked sixpence upon a crooked stile.
He bought a crooked cat, which caught a crooked mouse, and they all lived together in a little crooked house.

Trad.

Ye ho, little fishy don't cry, don't cry, ye ho, little fishy don't cry don't cry

Anon.

We wish you a merry Christmas…

Trad.

Old Chairs to Mend

If I'd as much money as I could spend,
I never would cry old chairs to mend.
Old chairs to mend, old chairs to mend,
I never would cry old chairs to mend.
If I'd as much money as I could tell,
I never would cry old clothes to sell.
Old clothes to sell, old clothes to sell;
I never would cry old clothes to sell.

Trad.

The quick witted cricket critic was critically injured.

Anon.

Six crisp snacks

Anon.

Crazy, crinkly, Christmas cracker wrapper

SD Burke

Three crooked cripples crawled through Cricklegate.

Anon.

Video:	https://youtu.be/tstIFmJIgH4
Audio:	https://audiomack.com/song/we_p/63-cr

	Video	Audio

Common Words, Names and Phrases		
crow	cross	Christopher
Christmas	create	Craig
cricket	crazy	Crystal
crown	cracked	Christine
cry	crude	Croatia
across	crisp	Christchurch
~to cry wolf~		
~as the crow flies~		
~crying crocodile tears~		
~cream of the crop~		
~up the creek~		

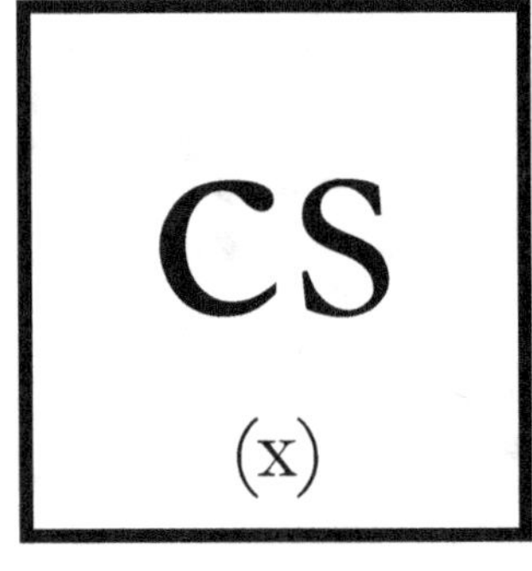

CS

(x)

Pope Sixtus the sixth's six texts.

Anon.

Sticks and stones may break my bones
But names will never hurt me.

Trad.

…Five six, pick up sticks…

Trad.

Fed Ex

Federal Express is now called FedEx. When I retire I'll be a FedEx ex.
But if I'm an officer when I retire, I'll be an ex Fedex Exec.
Then after a divorce, my ex-wife will be an ex FedEx exec's ex.
If I rejoin FedEx in time, I'd be an ex ex FedEx exec.
When we remarry, my wife will be an ex ex FedEx exec's ex.

Anon.

from **The Three Foxes**

Once upon a time there were three little foxes
Who didn't wear stockings, and they didn't wear sockses,
But they all had handkerchiefs to blow their noses,
And they kept their handkerchiefs in cardboard boxes…

AA Milne

Paddle Little Ducks

Paddle little ducks, paddle, paddle all day;
Paddle little ducks, paddle, paddle away.
-Five little ducks paddling to shore,
One paddled away, then there were four;
-Four little ducks paddling toward me,
One paddled away, then there were three;
-Three little ducks paddling toward you,
One paddled away, then there were two;
-Two little ducks paddling in the sun,
One paddled away, then there was one!

Trad.

Biscuit Box

A box of biscuits, a batch of mixed biscuits.
A box of biscuits for me to eat.
A box of mixed biscuits, a mixed biscuit box.
A box of mixed biscuits tastes better than old socks.

Anon.

Look for your socks in the odd socks box.

SD Burke

…If I were a merchant, I'd bring you six diamonds, with six blood red roses, for my love to wear…

J English

Common Words, Names and Phrases		
fox	excite	Max
box	explain	Alex
rocks	explore	Roxanne
accept	excellent	Rex
exercise	extra	Mexico
six	extreme	Texas
~think outside the box~ ~ as sly as a fox~ ~pull your socks up~ ~rocks in his head~ ~exit, stage left~		

Video: https://youtu.be/F0NIt-zHSGg		
Audio: https://audiomack.com/song/we_p/64-cs		
	Video	Audio

Hector Protector

Hector Protector was dressed all in green;
Hector Protector was sent to the Queen.
The Queen did not like him,
Nor did the King;
So Hector Protector was sent back again.

Trad.

Doctor!

If one doctor doctors another doctor, does
the doctor who doctors the doctor doctor the
doctor the way the doctor he is doctoring
doctors? Or does he doctor the doctor the
way that he, the doctor who is doctoring the
doctor, doctors?

Anon.

The instinct of an extinct insect stinks.

Anon.

Peter Piper

Peter Piper picked a peck of pickled peppers,
A peck of pickled peppers Peter Piper picked.
If Peter Piper picked a peck of pickled pep-
pers, where's the peck of pickled peppers
Peter Piper picked?

Anon.

from **I Was Only Nineteen**

…then someone yelled out "contact", and the
bloke behind me swore. We hooked in there
for hours, then a godalmighty roar. And
Frankie kicked a mine the day that mankind
kicked the moon. God help me, he was going
home in June…

J Schumann

I correctly recollect Rebecca MacGregor's
reckoning. I reckon I recollect correctly.

Anon.

Miss Polly Had a Dolly

Miss Polly had a dolly who was sick, sick, sick.
So she phoned for the doctor to be quick,
quick, quick.
The doctor came with his bag and his hat
And he knocked at the door with a rat-a-tat-
tat.
He looked at the dolly and he shook his head
And he said "Miss Polly, put her straight to
bed!"
He wrote on a paper for a pill, pill, pill
"I'll be back in the morning with my bill bill
bill."

Trad.

Video: https://youtu.be/_IfWrfI678M
Audio: https://audiomack.com/song/we_p/65-ct

	Video	Audio

Common Words, Names and Phrases		
October	picture	Octavia
factory	worked	Victor
impact	tactful	Hector
act	exact	Brookton
affect	correct	Acton
active	contact	Prospect
~respect is earned, not given~		
~packed like sardines~		
~they cooked the books~		
~he worked like a Trojan~		

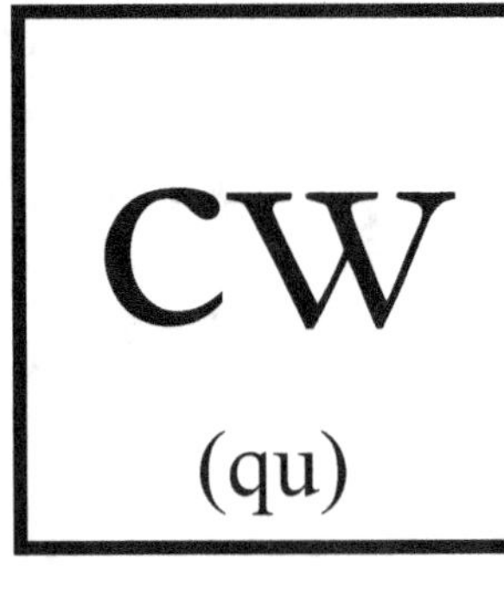

CW
(qu)

Quick kiss. Quicker kiss.

Anon.

Quiet, Quiet

Quiet, quiet, make not any noise.
Listen, listen to the Holy voice.
Wonder is now coming near,
Child of Light is coming here.
Quiet, quiet, make not any noise.

Trad.(German)

It is the dawning of the age of Aquarius, the age of Aquarius…. Aquarius… Aquarius…

J Rado & G Ragni

Queen Caroline

Queen, Queen Caroline,
Washed her hair in turpentine,
Turpentine made it shine,
Queen, Queen Caroline.

Trad.

Six Little Ducks

Six little ducks that I once knew
Fat ones, skinny ones, fair ones too
But the one little duck with a feather on his back
He led the others with a quack, quack, quack.
Quack, quack, quack! quack, quack, quack!
He led the others with a quack, quack, quack!...

Trad.

The Square Triangle

For any triangle that has a square angle
Pythagoras always felt fonder.
The sum of the squares of the two shorter
sides is the same as the square of the side that
is longer.
(Which longer side is the hypotenuse;
it faces the square angle, to aid the confused)
But remember this method can only be used
If your triangle has a square angle.

SD Burke

All the world is queer save thee and me, and even thou art a little queer

R Owen

Six quick quiz questions.

Anon.

Common Words, Names and Phrases		
queen	quote	Queenie
question	qualify	Quinn
quiz	quick	Quentin
require	quiet	Quince
quit	quite	Queensland
choir	square	Quebec
~call it quits~		
~the quick and the dead~		
~you need to watch the quiet ones~		
~to beg the question~		
~she's the queen bee~		

I Have a Little Dreidel

I have a little dreidel
I made it out of clay
And when it's dry and ready
Then dreidel I shall play!
    Oh – dreidel, dreidel, dreidel
    I made it out of clay
    And when it's dry and ready
    Then dreidel I shall play!
It has a lovely body
With legs so short and thin
And when my dreidel's tired
It drops and then I win!
    Oh – dreidel, dreidel, dreidel
    I made it out of clay
    And when it's dry and ready
    Then dreidel I shall play!

SS Grossman

How much dew would a dewdrop drop if a dewdrop could drop dew?

Anon.

From **The Rhyme of the Ancient Mariner**
…Water, water everywhere nor any drop to drink…

S Coleridge

I dropped it, I dropped it, on the way I dropped it. Someone must have picked it up and put it in my pocket….

Trad

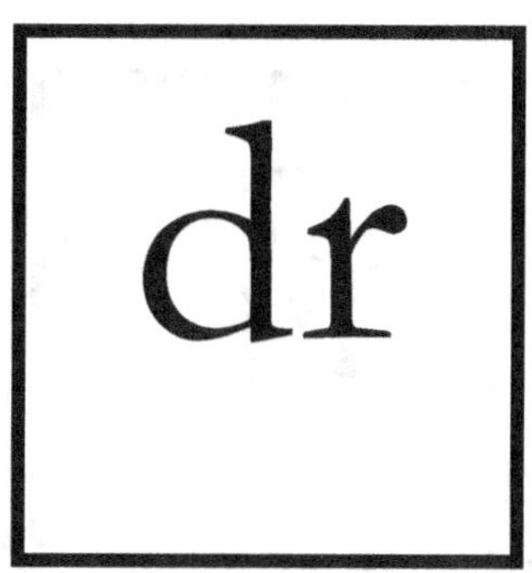

Draw drowsy ducks and drakes.
Draw them sitting in a lake.

Anon.

from **There's a Hole in the Bucket**
…But the stone is too dry, dear Liza, dear Liza, the stone is too dry, dear Liza, too dry..

Trad.

I think I'd like three drops of drink.

SD Burke

Only One Mother

Hundreds of stars in the pretty sky
Hundreds of shells on the shore together
Hundreds of birds that go singing by
Hundreds of lambs in the sunny weather
Hundreds of dewdrops to greet the dawn
Hundreds of bees in the purple clover
Hundreds of butterflies on the lawn
But only one mother the whole world over

G Cooper

Common Words, Names and Phrases		
drug	drop	Andrea
dragon	dry	Mildred
dream	dreadful	Deidre
drink	drowsy	Drake
drive	draw	Dresden
drain	dress	Drysdale

~drastic times call for drastic measures~
~he drinks like a fish~
~a drop in the ocean~
~all dressed up like a dog's dinner~
~he drives me bananas~

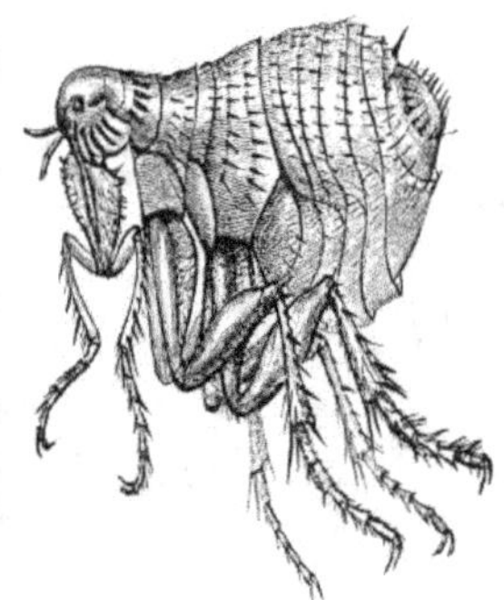

Fleas

Big fleas have little fleas,
Upon their backs to bite 'em,
And little fleas have lesser fleas,
and so, ad infinitum.
    And the great fleas, themselves, in turn
    Have greater fleas to go on;
    While these again have greater still,
    And greater still and so on.

after J Swift

Shoo! Fly, don't bother me. Shoo! Fly, don't
bother me. Shoo! Fly, don't bother me; I
don't want your company.

T Brigham-Bishop

From **You're a Grand old Flag**

You're a grand old flag, you're a high-flying
flag, you're a grand old flag though you're
torn to a rag, and forever in peace may you
wave…

GM Cohan

Little Peter Rabbit had a fly upon his nose…
so he flipped it and he flapped it and it flew
away.

Trad.

Video: https://youtu.be/nT4ksMafA2g	
Audio: https://audiomack.com/song/we_p/68-fl	

	Video	Audio

A Fly and a Flea in a Flue

A fly and a flea in a flue
Were imprisoned, so what could they do?
Said the fly, "Let us flee!"
"Let us fly!" said the flea.
So they flew through a flaw in the flue.

O Nash

Life is But a Melon

Life is butter, life is butter
melon cauliflower
melon cauliflower
Life is but a melon
Life is but a melon
cauliflower, cauliflower

Anon.

From **The Genesis Of The Butterfly**

…We dream that all white butterflies above,
Who seek through clouds or waters souls to
love,
And leave their lady mistress in despair,
To flit to flowers, as kinder and more fair,
Are but torn love-letters, that through the
skies
Flutter, and float, and change to butterflies.

V Hugo

Fat frogs flying past fast.
Fast fat flying frogs fly past fast.

Anon.

Common Words, Names and Phrases		
flower	flee	Florence
floor	fling	Floyd
flood	floppy	Fletcher
flag	flaccid	Flynn
fly	fluffy	Florida
flick	float	Flanders
~don't flog a dead horse~		
~it all came flooding back to me~		
~go fly a kite~		
~go down in flames~		
~flesh out the story~		

Flabby friars fly freely from France to flog
Frank's frogs.

SD Burke

Fresh French fried fly fritters

Anon.

Fred fed Ted bread, and Ted fed Fred bread.

Anon.

Five fat friars frying flat fish.
Five fat friars put them in a dish.

Anon.

A Frog Went a-Walking

A frog went a-walking on a summer's day, a-
hum. A frog went a-walking on a summer's
day, a-hum.   A frog went a-walking on a
summer's day, he met Miss Mousie on the
way, a-hum, a-hum, a-hum, a-hum….

Trad.(USA)

This Little Froggy

This little froggy took a big leap,
This little froggy took a small,
This little froggy leaped sideways,
And this little froggy not at all,
And this little froggy went,
Hippity, hippity, hippity hop, all the way
home.

Anon.

Fresh fried fish, Fish fresh fried, Fried fish
fresh, Fish fried fresh.

Anon.

I fry the end of my friend.
(spelling hint)

Anon.

Free, free, free Nelson Mandela!

J Dammers

From a Jack to a King. From loneliness to a
wedding ring. I played an Ace and I won a
Queen, and walked away with your heart.

N Miller

Frying Pan Theology

…Youngster says, "Frying Pan
What makes it snow?"
Frying Pan, confident,
Makes the reply --
"Shake 'im big flour bag
Up in the sky!" …

AB Paterson

Video: https://youtu.be/Y5DB1L0Ax6g		
Audio: https://audiomack.com/song/we_p/69-fr		
	Video	**Audio**

Common Words, Names and Phrases		
Friday	frown	Frank
frog	from	Frances
friend	fresh	Winifred
fry	frantic	Alfred
free	frost	France
fragrant	fray	Fremantle

~a frog in his throat~

~afraid of his shadow~

~fair weather friend~

~a friend in need is a friend indeed~

~out of the frying pan and into the fire~

gl

From **Little Snow White**
…Looking glass, looking glass on the wall
Who in this land is the fairest of all?...

Grimms

from **Sir Gawain and the Green Knight**
…which ever glimmered and glinted all with
green jewels…

Anon. 14C

from **The Empty Glass**
There are three lank bards in a borrowed
room—Ah! The number is one too few—
They have deemed their home and the bars
unfit
For the thing that they have to do.
Three glasses they fill with the Land's own
wine,
And the bread of life they pass.
Their glasses they take, which they slowly
raise—
And they drink to an empty glass…

H Lawson

Blue glue gun, green glue gun.

Anon.

Video: https://youtu.be/hnOYM7SaoDI
Audio: https://audiomack.com/song/we_p/70-gl

Video	Audio

The Glow-Worm
Shine little glow-worm, glimmer, glimmer
Shine little glow-worm, glimmer, glimmer…
Glow little glow-worm, fly of fire
Glow like an incandescent wire
Glow for the female of the species
Turn on the AC and the DC…
When you gotta glow, you gotta glow
Glow little glow-worm, glow

H Bolten-Backers

Glass
Words of a poem should be glass
But glass so simple-subtle its shape
Is nothing but the shape of what it holds.
  A glass spun for itself is empty,
  Brittle, at best Venetian trinket.
  Embossed glass hides the poem of its
  absence.
Words should be looked through, should be
windows.
The best word were invisible.
The poem is the thing the poet thinks.
  If the impossible were not,
  And if the glass, only the glass,
  Could be removed, the poem would
  remain.

R Francis

Green glass globes glow greenly.

Anon

Common Words, Names and Phrases		
glass	glance	Glenda
globe	glide	Glen
glove	glad	Douglas
glue	glum	Glenys
igloo	glossy	Glenelg
ugly	glutton	Glasgow
~ugly is as ugly does~ ~fits like a glove~ ~all that glitters is not gold~ ~people who live in glass houses shouldn't throw stones~ ~wearing his glad-rags~		

Ten Green Bottles

Ten green bottles sitting on the wall
Ten green bottles sitting on the wall
And if one green bottle should accidentally
fall, there'd be nine green bottles sitting on
the wall.
Nine green bottles…(etc.)….There'd be no
green bottles sitting on the wall.

Trad.

Some say the king's a great man and the emperor greater still, yet many say the greatest died on a lonely hill.

SD Burke

Some are born great, some achieve greatness, and some have greatness thrust upon them.

Shakespeare

Three grey geese in a green field grazing, grey were the geese and green was the grazing.

Anon.

The great Greek grape growers grow great Greek grapes.

Anon.

Great, green gobs of greasy, grimy gopher guts….

US, Anon.

How much ground could a groundhog grind if a groundhog could grind ground?

Anon.

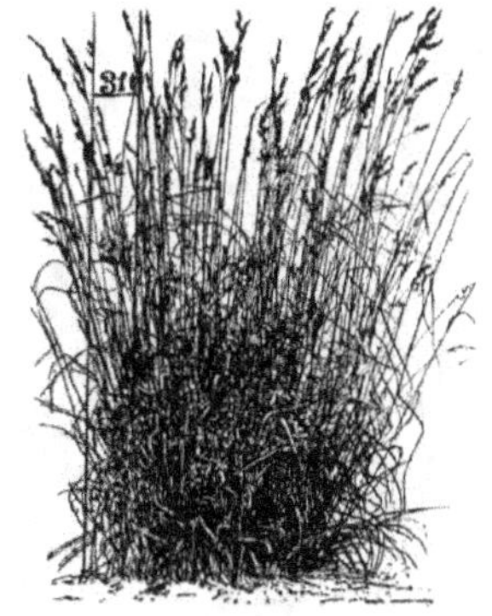

Green Grow the Rushes- Oh!

I'll sing you one ho!
Green grow the rushes oh!..

Trad.

If All the Seas Were One Sea

If all the seas were one sea,
What a great sea that would be!
And if all the trees were one tree,
What a great tree that would be!
And if all the axes were one axe,
What a great axe that would be!
And if all the men were one man,
What a great man he would be!
And if the great man took the great axe,
And cut down the great tree,
And let it fall into the great sea,
What a splish splash that would be!

Trad.

Common Words, Names and Phrases		
ground	grab	Grace
grandfather	great	Gretel
grass	grey	Margaret
grow	green	Greer
greet	agree	Greece
grapes	disgrace	Greenland

~the grass is always greener
on the other side of the hill~
~sour grapes~
~beware Greeks bearing gifts~
~green about the gills~
~growing like Topsy~

Video: https://youtu.be/imygV3NW1ik
Audio: https://audiomack.com/song/we_p/71-gr

	Video	Audio

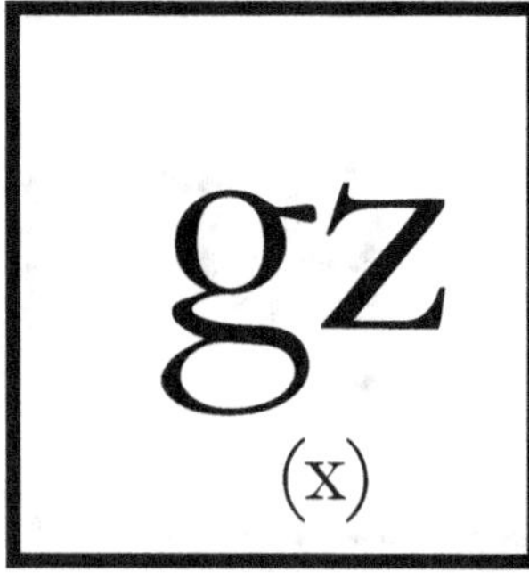

Lolly Legs Eleven

Lolly Legs Eleven could do seven at a trot
but he feared 'most any animal
and somehow he had got
   himself …stuck upon a farm
   and what should happen then but
   Pigs! Pigs! Pigs!
and Lolly Legs Eleven, on his pegs,
he did seven, and eleven, and a lot.
    2   …lost inside the woods
            Stags! Stags! Stags!
    3   …bogged down in a swamp
            Hogs! Hogs! Hogs!
    4   …locked outside at night
            Dogs! Dogs! Dogs!

SD Burke

Bandy Legs

As I was going to sell my eggs
I met a man with bandy legs,
Bandy legs and crooked toes;
I tripped up his heels, and he fell on his nose.

Trad.

Video: https://youtu.be/Cj-oC-_3TA0	
Audio: https://audiomack.com/song/we_p/72-gz	
	Video / Audio

Rotten Eggs

Eggs must be examined to see if they are fit
So place your eggs in water, whereby eggs
shall exhibit. The eggs that sink below the
waves are cause for exuberancy
But the ones that float, the rotten eggs, better
exiles be.

SD Burke

Earth Lag

The Earth lags just a little as it moves around
the Sun, and the Moon just tags along now
with the Earth upon its run.
The Moon lags just a little too, or that is what
I hear, and gets closer to exotic stars, some
40mill each year.
The Sun, type G example in the outer spiral
arm, exuberantly spirals outwards where it
might well come to harm.
Our Sun and Moon and Earth are all just cogs
in the cosmic night, but all a little legless, as if
something's not quite right.

SD Burke

Many Legs

Two legs sat upon three legs with one leg in
his lap ; In comes four legs and runs away
with one leg. Up jumps two legs catches up
three legs, throws it after four legs, and
makes him bring back one leg.

Anon.

Common Words, Names and Phrases		
exam	exist	Alexander
example	exotic	Alexandra
exile	exact	Pugsy
examine	exuberant	Exasperation
exaggerate	pegs	Inlet
~don't put all your eggs in one basket~		
~on his last legs~		
~as sure as eggs are eggs~		
~it's a mug's game~		

My Story's Ended

My story's ended,
My spoon is bended:
If you don't like it,
Go to the next door,
And get it mended.

Trad.

Old Chairs to Mend

If I'd as much money as I could spend,
I never would cry old chairs to mend ;
Old chairs to mend, old chairs to mend ;
I never would cry old chairs to mend.

Trad.

It would be handy to have a hundred hands, a
hundred hands would be handy.

SD Burke

Kind Hearts

Kind hearts are the gardens,
Kind thoughts are the roots
Kind words are the flowers
Kind deeds are the fruits
Take care of your garden
And keep out the weeds
Fill it with sunshine
Kind words and kind deeds

Longfellow

Hands on Shoulders

Hands on shoulders,
hands on knees.
Hands behind you,
if you please;
Touch your shoulders,
now your nose,
Now your hair and now your toes;
Hands up high in the air,
Down at your sides, and touch your hair;
Hands up high as before,
Now clap your hands, one-two-three-four!

Anon.

All a Row

All a row, a bendy bow,
Shoot at a pigeon and kill a crow;
Shoot at another and kill his brother;
Shoot again and kill a wren,
And that'll do for gentlemen.

Trad.

Common Words, Names and Phrases		
end	band	Andrea
under	bend	Glenda
stand	find	Andrew
hand	mind	Sandy
bond	lend	The Andes
trend	slender	Land's End
~the end of the line~		
~lend me your ears~		
~my word is my bond~		
~under the weather~		
~all's well that ends well~		

Video: https://youtu.be/tzgXE5Qmd4c

Audio: https://audiomack.com/song/we_p/73-nd

Video	Audio

If all the Land

If all the land were apple pie
And all the sea were ink
And all the trees were bread and cheese
What should we do for a drink?

Anon.

Five Little Monkeys

Five little monkeys jumping on the bed
One fell off and bumped his head
Mama called the doctor,
And the doctor said
No more monkeys jumping on the bed…

Trad.

If I Had a Donkey

If I had a donkey that wouldn't go
Do you think I'd beat him? Oh, no, no!
I'd put him in a barn and give him some corn,
The best little donkey that ever was born.

Trad. (USA)

Wynken, Blynken and Nod

Wynken, Blynken and Nod one night
Sailed off in a wooden shoe
Sailed on a river of crystal light
Into a sea of dew
"Where are you going and what do you
wish?"
The old moon asked the three
"We have come to fish for the herring fish
That live in this beautiful sea.
Nets of silver and gold have we!"
Said Wynken, Blynken and Nod…

E Field

from **I Love to Have a Beer with Duncan**

I love to have a beer with Duncan
Yeah, I love to have a beer with Dunc.
We drink in moderation
and we never ever ever get rolling drunk…

S Dusty

Little Donkey

Little donkey, little donkey on the dusty road
Got to keep on plodding onwards with your
precious load.
Been a long time, little donkey, through the
winter's night.
Don't give up now, little donkey,
Bethlehem's in sight…

E Boswell

Common Words, Names and Phrases		
bank	stink	Duncan
junk	pink	Frank
tank	clunky	Hank
think	lanky	Bianca
drink	thank	Lancashire
		Sanctuary Cove

~no need to thank me~
~you can take that to the bank~
~the monkey in me made me do it~
~as drunk as a skunk in a trunk~
~a nod's as good as a wink to a blind horse~

Incy Wincy Spider

Incy Wincy spider climbed up the water
spout. Down came the rain, and washed poor
Incy out
Out came the sun, and dried up all the rain
And Incy Wincy Spider climbed up the spout
again.

Trad.

from **I've Danced With a Man..**

I've danced with a man, who's danced with a
girl, who's danced with the Prince of Wales.
It was simply grand, he said "Topping band"
and she said "Delightful, Sir"
Glory, Glory, Alleluia! I'm the luckiest of fe-
males
For I've danced with a man, who's danced
with a girl, who's danced with the Prince of
Wales…

H Farjeon

from **Lord of the Dance**

I danced in the morning when the world was
begun
and I danced in the moon and the stars and
the sun
I came down from heaven and I danced on
the earth
At Bethlehem I had my birth
Dance, then, wherever you may be
I am the lord of the dance, said he
And I'll lead you all, wherever you may be
And I'll lead you all in the dance, said he…

S Carter

Fancy a dance, Nance?

Trad.

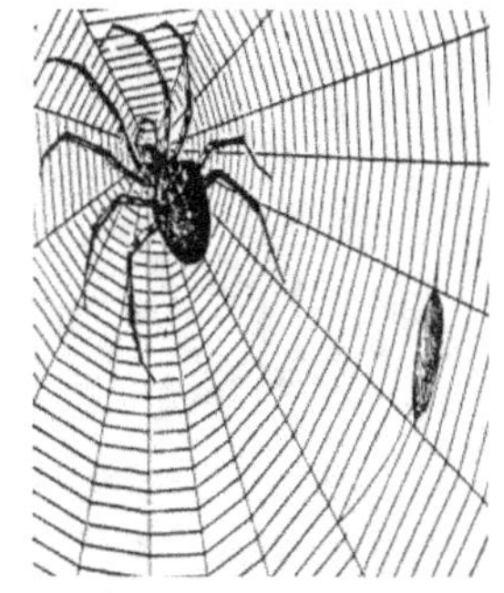

I Love Sixpence

I love sixpence, pretty little sixpence,
I love sixpence better than my life ;
I spent a penny of it, I spent another,
And took fourpence home to my wife.
    Oh, my little fourpence, pretty little four-
    pence,
    I love fourpence better than my life ;
    I spent a penny of it, I spent another,
    And I took twopence home to my wife.
Oh, my little twopence, my pretty little two-
pence,
I love twopence better than my life ;
I spent a penny of it, I spent another,
And I took nothing home to my wife.
    Oh, my little nothing, my pretty little noth-
    ing,
    What will nothing buy for my wife ?
    I have nothing, I spend nothing,
    I love nothing better than my wife.

Trad.

Common Words, Names and Phrases		
ransom	dance	Nancy
dunce	once	Constance
prince	fancy	Spencer
answer	since	Winston
rinse	balance	France
incense	ambulance	Florence

~once bitten, twice shy~
~the inside scoop~
~ants in your pants~
~a king's ransom~
~a prince among men~

Video:	https://youtu.be/cE1n-QtHkPA
Audio:	https://audiomack.com/song/we_p/75-ns

	Video	Audio

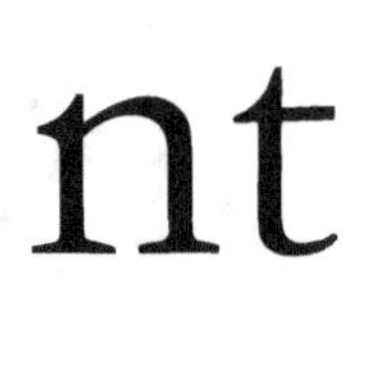

nt

Not everything that can be counted counts, and not everything that counts can be counted.

WB Cameron

For Want of a Nail
For want of a nail, the shoe was lost;
For want of the shoe, the horse was lost;
For want of the horse, the rider was lost;
For want of the rider, the battle was lost;
For want of the battle, the kingdom was lost,
And all for the want of a horseshoe nail.

Trad.

The Ant and the Elephant
Said a tiny Ant   To the Elephant
"Mind how you tread in this clearing!"
But alas! Cruel fate!
She was crushed by the weight
Of an Elephant, hard of hearing.

S Milligan

Clement spent the interim doing a stint at the Parliament Apartments, conveniently centered adjacent to the Parliament.

SD Burke

Video: https://youtu.be/cJrrOnEaMW8
Audio: https://audiomack.com/song/we_p/76-nt

	Video	Audio

An antelope can't elope with a cantelope.

Anon.

He Couldn't
He laughed when they said it couldn't be done. He smiled and said he knew it.
But he tried the thing that couldn't be done,
And found he couldn't do it.

Anon.

Penny, penny, easily spent.
Copper brown and worth one cent.

Anon.

The Aunts
There were three sisters in a hall,
There came a knight amongst them all ;
"Good morrow, Aunt," to the one,
"Good morrow, Aunt," to the other,
"Good morrow, Gentlewoman," to the third,
"If you were my aunt, as the other two be, I would say good morrow, then, aunts, all three."

Trad.

Willie Sent Millicent
The bottle of perfume that Willy sent
was highly displeasing to Millicent.
Her thanks were so cold
that they quarreled, I'm told
over that silly scent Willy sent Millicent

Anon.

Now is the winter of our discontent…

Shakespeare

Common Words, Names and Phrases		
don't	went	Clint
can't	want	Antonia
different	enter	Santa Claus
government	into	Bunty
bent	sent	Levant
hunt	won't	Kent
~different strokes for different folks~		
~can't stand it~		
~sent to Coventry~		
~count your blessings~		
~independently wealthy~		

Paul Plymouth

Paul Plymouth plays piano pieces pleasantly
With aplomb, and at the slightest cause,
And we plead with him, "Paul Plymouth,
please,
Please, please pause for proper applause!"

SD Burke

Diddle Diddle Dumpling

Diddle, diddle, dumpling, my son John,
Went to bed with his trousers on;
One shoe off, and the other shoe on,
Diddle, diddle, dumpling, my son John.

Trad.

Bring a Plate

At a party antipodean
You're asked *"please bring a plate"*
And, yes, this does mean choosing
A single plate from many plates
But before you spend too much time
Discerning just which plate is great
(a trial which might just plausibly
see you running late)
Please remember that no matter
the pleasant patina, hue or state
    If your platter shows up vacant
    If it lacks a certain something
    If it's empty
    It's not pleasant
And you haven't brought a plate.

SD Burke

Father Placid's pleasant priests play and pray,
pray and play, play and pray all day.

SD Burke

The Dumplings

Pussy-cat ate the dumplings, the dumplings,
Pussy-cat atc thc dumplings.
Mamma stood by, and cried, "Oh, fie!
Why did you eat the dumplings?"

Trad.

Oonagh's Plaits

She placed one plait around her wrist
One plait around her ankle placed
Plait three, itself, circled her heart
And, so fortified, her plans could start
Now none of her efforts would go to waste
And she readied herself for the tryst.

SD Burke

Common Words, Names and Phrases		
place	plan	Placid
plane	plain	Plato
plant	plump	Pleasance
play	pleasant	Ripley
reply	apply	Plymouth
replace	plastic	Plano
~pull the plug~ ~he's pleasant enough~ ~it's plain to see~ ~play hookey~ ~there's no place like home~		

Video: https://youtu.be/ASyF26np0I8

Audio: https://audiomack.com/song/we_p/77-pl

Video	Audio

Proper Cup of Coffee

What I want is a proper cup of coffee made in a proper cup of coffee pot. I may be off my dot but I do want a proper cup of coffee made in a proper cup of coffee pot. Tin coffee pots and iron coffee pots, they're no use to me. If I can't have a proper cup of coffee made in a proper cup of coffee pot, I'll have a cup of tea.

R Weston & W Lee

The Pirate's Private Property

Anon.

Practically Perfect

If practice makes perfect and perfect needs practice, I'm perfectly practised and practically perfect.

Anon.

Our children need our presence more than our presents.

Anon.

Proper prior preparation prevents poor performance.

Anon.

Video: https://youtu.be/6jSO_K3YRKo		
Audio: https://audiomack.com/song/we_p/78-pr		
	Video	**Audio**

From **The Frog Prince**

…Princess! youngest Princess! Open the door to me.
Do you not know what you said to me
Yesterday by the cool waters of the well?
Princess! youngest Princess! Open the door to me…

Grimm

Where are you going to, my pretty maid?
Where are you going to, my pretty maid?..

Trad.

Betty Pringle's Pig

Did you not hear of Betty Pringle's pig ?
It was not very little, nor yet very big ;
The pig sat down upon a dunghill,
And then poor piggy he made his will.
Betty Pringle came to see this pretty pig,
That was not very little, nor yet very big ;
This little piggy it lay down and died,
And Betty Pringle sat down and cried.
Then Johnny Pringle buried this very pretty pig,
That was not very little, nor yet very big ;
So here's an end of the song of all three,
Johnny Pringle, Betty Pringle, and the little Piggie.

Trad.

A practical but pretty expensive present.

M Ponsonby

Common Words, Names and Phrases		
pram	practise	Princess
prawn	prick	Priya
pretty	precious	Primrose
prisoner	imprecise	Priscilla
pray	pregnant	Prague
prepare	impress	Pretoria

~practice makes perfect~

~sitting pretty~

~the proof is in the pudding~

~dressed to impress~

~ a pregnant pause~

Earthside

One System, One People,
No accident of birth
But whenever you vis' me, Cousin,
I learn well my lessers
By the stark light of Earth.
Lesser air, lesser water,
Lesser gravity, lesser girth.
    Fourth from the sun
    And no Constitution
    Can assure us of our worth
    The Mars-born, the red-men,
    The thin-boned pioneers
    Our birthright
    is dust
And so you must
Forgive me if I don't feel
What you feel
The greeny-blueness that you feel
When you say you'll see me
    Earthside.

SD Burke

Under the Earth

Under the earth, a dearth of light
A dearth of mirth, no need for sight
There the worm turns, in the endless night
Under the dark, dark earth.

SD Burke

Happy Birthday

Happy Birthday to you
Happy Birthday to you
Happy Birthday dear, ______
Happy Birthday to you

Trad.

Video: https://youtu.be/vIPkG_1eT9A
Audio: https://audiomack.com/song/we_p/79-rth

	Video	Audio

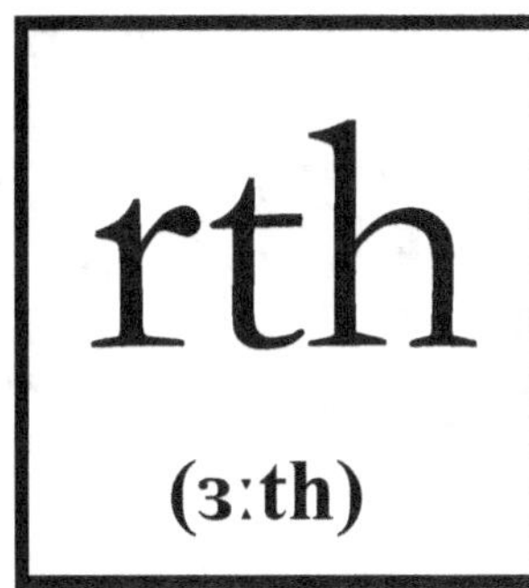

rth
(3:th)

Happy Birthday, Sun and Moon

Happy birthday, happy birthday,
Many, many happy returns
Happy birthday, happy birthday
Sun and moon and stars rejoice
Upon your birthday, upon your birthday
While we join hands in a ring and sing

Waldorf Schools

The Young Fellow From Perth

There was a young fellow from Perth
Who was born on the day of his birth
He was married, they say,
On his wife's wedding day
And he died when he quitted this earth.

Anon.

Common Words, Names and Phrases		
birth	worth	Bertha
birthday	fourth	Arthur
earth	mirth	Martha
hearth	north	Darth
unearth	arthritis	Perth
orthodox	swarthy	Earth

~worth every penny~
~cost the earth~
~the salt of the earth~
~he's worth his salt~
~doesn't know if he's Arthur or Martha~

sk

Skip to my Lou

Be my darling, skip to my Lou
Be my darling, skip to my Lou
Be my darling, skip to my Lou
Skip to my Lou, my darling...

Trad. (USA)

The Cat Spat

The cat spat and scratched me
He scratched me he scratched me
He scratched me on the esplanade
The esplanade, the esplanade
Bad luck that cat who spat and scratched
He scratched me on the esplanade

SD Burke

The Man in Thessaly

There was a man in Thessaly,
    And he was wondrous wise,
He jumped into a quickset hedge.
    And scratched out both his eyes;
And when he saw his eyes were out,
    And he was in great pain,
He jumped into a holly bush,
    And scratched them in again.

Trad.

Video: https://youtu.be/_ArWemKpO24

Audio: https://audiomack.com/song/we_p/80-sk

Video	Audio

Silly scorpions ski incessantly.

Anon.

Skillful Smith, the Skatepark Hero

Skillful Smith, the skatepark hero
He's the king of the scooter flip
Backflip
Frontflip
Heigh ho, dip dip
The skatepark hero
Skillful Smith
    Skillful Smith, the skatepark hero,
    he's the king of the scooter flip.
    Inward, bar spin
    (gotta keep your arms in)
    -the skatepark hero,
    Skillful Smith.
Skillful Smith, the skatepark hero,
he's the king of the scooter flip.
Skillful- no clip,
eyes wide –tailwhip!
-the skatepark hero,
Skillful Smith.
    Skillful Smith, the skatepark hero,
    he's the king of the scooter flip.
    540! (by a hair),
    not scared –didn't care,
    -the skatepark hero,
    Skillful Smith.
Skillful Smith, the skatepark hero,
he's the king of the scooter flip.

SD Burke

Common Words, Names and Phrases		
sky	ski	Oscar
squirrel	skip	Scarlett
ask	scared	Scott
skeleton	school	Skye
skyscraper	skeptical	Scandinavia
	describe	Scotland

~by the skin of his teeth~
~start from scratch~
~scratch my back and I'll scratch yours~
~no skin off my nose~
~as skinny as a rake~

from **Rhyme of the Ancient Mariner**

…Oh sleep! it is a gentle thing,
Beloved from pole to pole!
To Mary Queen the praise be given!
She sent the gentle sleep from Heaven,
That slid into my soul…

S Coleridge

Go to Sleep My Baby

Go to sleep my baby
Close your pretty eyes
Angels up above you
Look down on you from the sky.
Great big moon is shining
Stars begin to peep
It's time for all the tiny babies
To go to sleep…

Trad.

Come, Let's to Bed

"To bed! To bed!"
Said Sleepy-head;
"Tarry awhile," said Slow;
"Put on the pan,"
Said Greedy Nan;
"We'll sup before we go."

Trad.

Slip, slop, slap. Slip on a shirt, slop on sun-screen and slap on a hat…

Cancer Council, Victoria

Six slick slimy snails slowly slithering south-wards.

Anon.

Sleep Baby, Sleep

Sleep, baby, sleep
Your father tends the sheep
Your mother shakes the dreamland tree
And from it fall sweet dreams for thee
Sleep, baby, sleep
Sleep, baby, sleep

    Sleep, baby, sleep
    Our cottage vale is deep
    The little lamb is on the green
    With snowy fleece so soft and clean
    Sleep, baby, sleep
    Sleep, baby, sleep

Trad.

Are you Sleeping?

Are you sleeping, are you sleeping?
Brother John, Brother John,
Morning bells are ringing
Morning bells are ringing
Ding dang dong, ding dang dong.

Trad. (French)

Common Words, Names and Phrases		
slab	slide	Ainslie
slob	slow	Slade
slave	sleek	Sloane
sleep	slippery	Slater
slip	asleep	Slovenia
priceless	slimy	Slough

~a slap in the face~
~a slip of the tongue~
~ a slave to love~
~slowly, slowly, catch the monkey~
~it's a slippery slope~

Video: https://youtu.be/DLLue35CFfk
Audio: https://audiomack.com/song/we_p/81-sl

	Video	Audio
Wonderful English		

The Sneeze

I sneezed a sneeze into the air
It fell to earth I know not where
But hard and froze were the looks of those
In whose vicinity I snoze

Anon.

There was a Little Turtle

There was a little turtle
Who lived in a box.
He swam in puddles
And climbed on rocks.
He snapped at the mosquito,
He snapped at the flea.
He snapped at the minnow,
And he snapped at me.
He caught the mosquito,
He caught the flea.
He caught the minnow,
But he didn't catch me!

V Lindsay

Snips and snails and puppy dog's tails, that's
what little boys are made of.

Trad.

Video: https://youtu.be/xLn-AWZiy6Y
Audio: https://audiomack.com/song/we_p/82-sn

	Video	Audio
Wonderful English		

Snowflakes

Snowflakes are falling by ones and twos
There's snow on my jacket, and snow on my shoes
There's snow on the bushes and snow on the trees
It's snowing on everything now if you please.

LF Jackson

Sneeze on a Monday

If you sneeze on Monday, you sneeze for danger;
Sneeze on a Tuesday, kiss a stranger;
Sneeze on a Wednesday, sneeze for a letter;
Sneeze on a Thursday, something better;
Sneeze on a Friday, sneeze for sorrow;
Sneeze on a Saturday, see your sweetheart to-morrow

Trad.

The Monkeys and the Crocodile

Five little monkeys swinging from a tree
Teasing Mr. Crocodile, "You can't catch me!"
Here comes Mr. Crocodile, as quiet as can be
And snatch that monkey right out of that tree!
Four little Monkeys swinging from a tree…
…and snatch that monkey right out of that tree!
…No more monkeys!

Trad.

Common Words, Names and Phrases		
snail	snow	Snowdon
snack	snobby	Snowy
snake	sneaky	Snape
snip	snug	Sneem
sneak	snide	Snook
snob	ensnare	Snowball
~it's nothing to sneeze at~		
~he's a snake in the grass~		
~as slow as a snail~		
~snug as a bug in a rug~		
~they did a snow job on him~		

The Bird's Nest

I've heard it's true in China
They've a dish of sparrow spit
Some sort of spicy speciality
Is what I've heard of it
But it'll be a pretty special day
When I eat what sparrows spat
I'd rather spend a year on spuds
Than have a go at that.

SD Burke

I spy with my little eye
Something beginning with____

Trad.

Incy Wincy Spider

Incy Wincy spider climbed up the water spout. Down came the rain, and washed the spider out.
Out came the sun, and dried up all the rain
And Incy Wincy Spider climbed up the spout again.

Trad.

Little Cock Sparrow

A little cock sparrow sat on a tree,
Looking as happy, as happy could be,
Till a boy came by with his bow and arrow:
Says he, "I will shoot the little cock sparrow…"

Trad.

Pease porridge hot, pease porridge cold,
 Pease porridge in the pot, nine days old…

Trad.

Five Little Speckled Frogs

Five little speckled frogs
Sat on a speckled log
Eating the most delicious bugs
   Yum yum
One jumped into the pool
Where it was nice and cool
Then there were four green speckled frogs…

Anon.

Split Pea Broth

2 cups of split peas; splish, splash and drain
1 large onion, split a thousand ways
1 large leek, split up and spliced
1 large carrot, splendidly diced
1 clove of garlic, splayed if you like
A little salt and pepper, to make it very nice
2 stalks of celery, leaves on or off
Simmer it for hours, taking off the froth
Stirring splendour, splutter, splatter,
(add smoked meat? - it doesn't matter)
-Split Pea Broth!!

SD Burke

Common Words, Names and Phrases		
spoon	spit	Spencer
space	speak	Hesperia
spider	spicy	Espen
spy	spare	Asberger
aspect	spoilt	Spain
perspire	spade	Split

~to spill the beans~
~on the spur of the moment~
~speak of the devil~
~spare the rod and spoil the child~
~spick and span~

Video: https://youtu.be/IaZ4mY17SRU
Audio: https://audiomack.com/song/we_p/83-sp

	Video	Audio

Spring Fairy

Spring Fairy wakes from Winter's halls
And sprightly springs but then she falls
Too fat by far, she twists her knee
And sprains her ankle, and so we see
That if too much
Pleasure is wrung
From Winter's bed
 -our spring is sprung!

SD Burke

Brussel Sprouts

Brussel Sprouts, eaten fresh
Are very nice indeed.
And yesterday's sprouts might yet still be
Fit for a pleasant feed.
And if you chop them finely
They make a lovely spread
But eat them old, those Brussel Sprouts
And then you'll wish you were dead.

SD Burke

Widespread rioting, widespread rioting.

Anon.

Jack Sprat

Jack Sprat could eat no fat.
His wife could eat no lean.
And so between them both, you see,
They licked the platter clean.

Trad.

Until Disproven

Innocent until guilt is proven?
How quaint, no, no,
The reverse applies.
A mainspring, you say
Of jurisprudence?
Come, come, now Sir,
Our law is spry
For here we cast out such a mackerel
That no sprat can get away
In any event, it's plain to see
This man's as guilty as the day!

SD Burke

Spring Time

…In spring time, in spring time, the only pretty ring time,
When birds do sing, Hey ding a ding, ding:
Hey ding a ding, ding Hey ding a ding, ding
Sweet lovers love the spring…

Shakespeare

Far out, Brussel Sprout!

Trad.(Aust)

Video: https://youtu.be/mpJ0haT4NSU
Audio: https://audiomack.com/song/we_p/84-spr

Video	Audio

Common Words, Names and Phrases		
spring	spread	Sprat
sprat	spry	Springsteen
spree	spruced	Esprit
spray	springy	Springfield
sprain	sprout	Spratly Is.
spritely	offspring	Alice Springs
~spread too thinly~		
~a sprat to catch a mackerel~		
~a spring in her step~		
~the first swallow of Spring~		
~no spring chicken~		

There is a Stone

There is a stone stands in the sea,
A heavy rock, a fine stone,
A lonely stone, it stands alone,
It stands and yearns to be free,
And the waves whip along….

SD Burke

Stuck Fast

Will you stay by my side?
Be my first and my last?
Will you storm my Bastille
And reach for my stars?
Will you stick with me always?
My straight arrow true
Stray never and nowhere
Ah! Fantastic You!

SD Burke

A maid with a duster made a furious bluster
Dusting a bust in the hall.
When the bust it was dusted the bust it was
busted. The bust it was dust, that's all.

Anon

We Three Kings

…Star of wonder, star of night,
Star with royal beauty bright
Westward leading, still proceeding
Guide us to thy perfect light…

JH Hopkins

…Every gal in Constantinople
Lives in Istanbul, not Constantinople
So if you've a date in Constantinople
She'll be waiting in Istanbul…

J Kennedy

from **Sea Fever**

I must go down to the seas again, to the lonely sea and the sky. And all I ask is a tall ship
and a star to steer her by…

J Masefield

One flew east and one flew west,
And one flew over the cuckoo's nest.

Trad.

Star light, star bright, first star I see tonight;
I wish I may, I wish I might, have the wish I
wish tonight.

Trad.

North, South, East, West,
Home is best, home is best.

Trad.

Stupid superstition!

Anon.

Sticks and stones may break my bones but
names will never hurt me.

Trad.

Common Words, Names and Phrases		
stars	stick	Steve
sister	sting	Stacey
start	nest	Stuart
cost	must	Austin
stand	rest	Estonia
stay	stop	Istanbul

~a fault confessed is half redressed~
~it's the last straw~
~a storm in a teacup~
~in a stew~
~a stiff upper lip~

str

The strong stocky soccer striker struck the stretchy net.

SD Burke

String, string, string, string, everybody loves string…

B Oddie

Turkey in the Straw

…Turkey in the straw
Turkey in the straw
Roll 'em up and twist 'em up
A high tuck a-haw
And hit 'em up a tune called
Turkey in the Straw…

Trad (USA)

from **There's a Hole in the Bucket**

…With straw, Dear Henry, Dear Henry, Dear Henry, with straw, Dear Henry, Dear Henry, with straw.
But the straw is too long, Dear Liza, Dear Liza, the straw is too long, Dear Liza, too long…

Trad.

Tommy Trot

Tommy Trot, a man of law,
Sold his bed and lay upon straw,
Sold the straw and slept on grass
To buy his wife a looking-glass.

Trad.

A Beetle and a Broom Straw

A robin and a wren, as they walked along one night,
Saw a big brown beetle on a broom straw.
Said the robin to the wren: "What a pretty, pretty sight, that big brown beetle on a broom straw!?"
So they got their plates and knives,
Their children and their wives,
And gobbled up the beetle on the broom straw.

Trad.

Jack Straw's Castle

Jack Straw laid down the law
And vowed there was nothing for building like straw
He built him a castle in less than a day.
Its walls were of stubble its roof was of hay
A capful of wind flew out of the shaw
And blew down his castle and blew up Jack Straw.

E Farjeon

Video: https://youtu.be/xlR1nO4dPKo		
Audio: https://audiomack.com/song/we_p/86-str		
	Video	Audio

Common Words, Names and Phrases		
string	struggle	Astrid
street	strong	Astro
stream	strange	Istria
stretch	straight	Australia
strike	astronomy	Stratford
abstract	ancestry	Stroud
~as strong as an ox~		
~as straight as a die~		
~the last straw~		
~pull some strings~		
~strike while the iron is hot~		

Swing Me Over the Water

Swing me over the water
Swing me over the sea
Swing me over the garden wall
And swing me home for tea.

Trad.

Swing Low, Sweet Chariot.

Swing low, sweet chariot
Coming for to carry me home
Swing low, sweet chariot
Coming for to carry me home…

W Willis?

Bees

A swarm of bees in May is worth a load of hay; A swarm of bees in June is worth a silver spoon; A swarm of bees in July is not worth a fly.

Trad.

Swanee

Swanee, how I love you, how I love you
My dear old Swanee.
I give the world to be
Among the folks in D-I-X-I-E
Even though my mammy's
Waiting for me, Praying for me
Down by the Swanee.
The folks up north will see me no more
When I get to that Swanee shore. …

I Caesar

Swan Swam

Swan swam over the sea. Swim, swan, swim!
Swan swam back again. Well swum, swan!

Anon.

Video: https://youtu.be/ItpOENoHJT4

Audio: https://audiomack.com/song/we_p/87-sw

	Video	Audio

Saint Swithin's Day

St. Swithin's day if thou dost rain
For forty days it will remain
St. Swithin's day, if thou be fair
For forty days 'twill rain no more.

Trad.

There was an old woman who swallowed a fly.

There was an old woman who swallowed a fly. I don't know why she swallowed a fly. Perhaps she'll die.

There was an old woman who swallowed a spider. That wriggled and jiggled and wiggled inside her.
She swallowed the spider to catch the fly.
I don't know why she swallowed the fly. Perhaps she'll die...

Trad.

Common Words, Names and Phrases		
swan	swallow	Swannee
swamp	sweet	Swithin
swine	swiftly	Sweetheart
sweep	swollen	Swansea
sweat	swim	Swaziland
swell	swarm	Sweden
~don't sweat the small stuff~		
~swallow your pride~		
~in full swing~		
~sink or swim~		
~the sweet smell of success~		

Theophilus Thistle

On three thousand acres, too tangled for till-
ing, where three thousand thorn trees grew
thrifty and thrilling, Theophilus Thistle, less
thrifty than some, thrust three thousand thistles through the thick of his thumb!

Anon.

Three Young Rats

Three young rats with black felt hats,
Three young ducks with white straw flats,
Three young dogs with curling tails,
Three young cats with demi-veils,
   Went out to walk with two young pigs
   In satin vests and sorrel wigs.
   But suddenly it began to rain
   And so they all went home again

Trad.

Theo's throat throbs and thumps, thumps and
throbs.

Anon..

He threw three balls against the wall.
Three balls against the wall he threw.

Anon.

Oonagh's Plan

Once thrice threaded the thread three times,
about her ankle, wrist and heart
She swiftly, thriftily, thought of a plan
-the thread thrice threaded aided her art.

SD Burke

Fred Threlfall's thirty-five fine threads are fin-
er threads than Fred Threlfall's thirty-five
thick threads.

Anon.

He threw three free throws.

Anon.

He That Would Thrive

He that would thrive
Must rise at five;
He that hath thriven
May lie till seven;
And he that by the plough would thrive,
Himself must either hold or drive.

Trad.

The Three Ravens

There were three ravens sat on a tree
Down a down, hey down, hey down
There were three ravens sat on a tree,
 with a down
There were three ravens sat on a tree
They were as black as they might be
With a down, derry, derry derry down
down…

Trad.

Common Words, Names and Phrases		
throat	thrill	Catherine
throne	thrice	Kathryn
throng	three	Thrushbeard
throw	thrifty	Thring
thread	birthrate	Thrapston
thrust	enthrall	Thredbo

~don't throw good money after bad~
~throw the book at them~
~throw in the towel~
~the thrill of the chase~
~to lose the thread~

Video: https://youtu.be/nTMwgp_T6rw

Audio: https://audiomack.com/song/we_p/88-thr

	Video	Audio

Trick or Treat

Trick or Treat! Trick or Treat!
Give me something good to eat.
Give me candy. Give me cake.
Give me something sweet to take!

Anon.

Tricky Tristan

Tricky Tristan tracked a trail of tiny turtles.
How many tiny turtles did Tricky Tristan
track?
Tricky Tristan tracked twenty two tiny turtles;
That's how many tiny turtles tricky Tristan
tracked.

Anon.

On the first day of Christmas my true love
gave to me.. a partridge in a pear tree…

Trad.

I Had a Little Nut Tree

I had a little nut tree,
Nothing would it bear
But a silver nutmeg
And a golden pear.
    The King of Spain's daughter
    Came to visit me
    and all for the sake
    Of my little nut tree!..

Trad.

Where You There?

…Oh, oh, oh, oh, sometimes it causes me to
tremble, tremble, tremble…
Were you there when they crucified my
Lord?...

Trad.(USA)

This is the Way

This is the way the ladies ride,
Tri, tre, tre, tree,
Tri, tre, tre, tree!
This is the way the ladies ride,
Tri, tre, tre, tree, tri-tre-tre-tree!
This is the way the gentlemen ride,
Gallop-a-trot,
Gallop-a-trot!
This is the way the gentlemen ride,
Gallop-a-gallop-a-trot!
This is the way the farmers ride,
Hobbledy-hoy,
Hobbledy-hoy!
This is the way the farmers ride,
Hobbledy-hobbledy-hoy
And down into a ditch!

Trad.

Video: https://youtu.be/oveKmfGzbYg
Audio: https://audiomack.com/song/we_p/89-tr

	Video	Audio
Wonderful English		

Common Words, Names and Phrases		
truck	try	Patrick
tree	trade	Tricia
train	tricky	Tran
trap	true	Tristan
trick	tropical	Trinidad
retreat	retry	Eritrea
~if at first you don't succeed, try and try again~		
~tricks of the trade~		
~one man's trash is another's treasure~		
~can't see the wood for the trees~		
~Beauty is Truth, Truth: Beauty~		

ts

The Queen of Hearts

The queen of hearts, she made some tarts
All on a summer's day
The knave of hearts, he stole the tarts, and
took them clean away
The king of hearts called for the tarts
And beat the knave full sore
The knave of hearts brought back the tarts
And vowed he'd steal no more

Trad.

from **The Pied Piper**

…Rats!
They fought the dogs and killed the cats,
And bit the babies in the cradles,
And ate the cheeses out of the vats,
And licked the soup from the cooks' own la-
dles,
Split open the kegs of salted sprats,
Made nests inside men's Sunday hats,
And even spoiled the women's chats,
By drowning their speaking
With shrieking and squeaking
In fifty different sharps and flats…

R Browning

Amidst the Mists

Amidst the mists and coldest frosts,
with stoutest wrists and loudest boasts,
he thrusts his fist against the posts
and still insists he sees the ghosts.

Anon.

It's Raining, it's Pouring

It's raining, it's pouring,
The old man is snoring
Went to bed, bumped his head
And couldn't get up in the morning.

Trad.

Nuts in May

Here we go gathering nuts in May,
Nuts in May, nuts in May,
Here we go gathering nuts in May,
On a cold and frosty morning.
    Who will you have for nuts in May,
    Nuts in May, nuts in May,
    Who will you have for nuts in May,
    On a cold and frosty morning.
We'll have [name] for nuts in May,
Nuts in May, nuts in May,
We'll have [name] for nuts in May,
On a cold and frosty morning.

Trad.

Video: https://youtu.be/VDNBUitfvXM
Audio: https://audiomack.com/song/we_p/90-ts

	Video	Audio

Common Words, Names and Phrases		
rats	starts	Patsy
objects	parts	Whatsisname
it's	abuts	Hutson
its	treats	Abbottsford
nuts	bets	Watson's Bay
hats	meets	Mounts Bay

~eats like a bird~
~stir up a hornet's nest~
~what's done is done~
~it's an ill wind that blows no good~
~one man's meat's another man's poison~

Twinkle, Twinkle, Little Star

Twinkle, twinkle, little star,
How I wonder what you are.
Up above the world so high,
Like a diamond in the sky.
Twinkle, twinkle, little star,
How I wonder what you are.

J Taylor

The Twister of Twists

When a twister twisting would twist him a
twist,
For twisting a twist three twists he will twist ;
But if one of the twists untwists from the
twist,
The twist untwisting untwists the twist.

Trad.

Twice Two

Twice twelve is twenty four
Twice twenty's forty
The numbers can't add up to more
They can't be slack or naughty
It doesn't matter what you do
Or how you try to seek it
Twice two is only four
No matter how you tweak it.

SD Burke

Tweedledum and Tweedledee

Tweedledum and Tweedledee
Agreed to have a battle
For Tweedledum said Tweedledee
Had spoiled his nice new rattle.

Trad

Video: https://youtu.be/tXqluttPuMY
Audio: https://audiomack.com/song/we_p/91-tw

	Video	Audio

All the little birds on Jaybird Street love to
hear the robin go *tweet tweet tweet*. Rockin' Robin…

L Rene`

Pairs or Pears

Twelve pairs hanging high,
Twelve knights riding by,
Each knight took a pear,
And yet left a dozen there.

Trad.

Cows Eat Wheat

Cows eat wheat and sows eat wheat and little
bears eat honey. Bees'll eat honey, too,
wouldn't you?
(Cowsytweet and sowsytweet and little bearsy-
tunny, beeslytunny too wouldn't you?)

Anon.

Common Words, Names and Phrases		
twig	twitter	Twain
twin	between	Twyla
twine	twice	Twiggy
twist	twisted	Tweety Bird
twirl	twining	Twin Peaks
tweed	twinning	Twyford
~once bitten, twice shy~		
~don't twist my words~		
~a twinkle in his eye~		
~fool me once, shame on you.		
Fool me twice, shame on me~		
~between a rock and a hard place~		

IV

SILENT LETTERS

Silent A

aesthetic, bread, publically, logically, musically, romantically…

Fresh Baked Bread

Fresh baked bread is a yummy treat,
Filled with love and warmth and wheat,
Knead the dough and let it rise,
And soon you'll have a big surprise,
From the water, flour, and yeast,
Grows a golden, delicious feast.

Anon.

and see **Peas Porridge Hot** and **Five Plump Peas,** on page 12

Silent B

debt, plumber, lamb, climb, comb, crumb, dumb, doubt. numb, limb, subtle, thumb, tomb, womb…

Young Lambs to Sell

Young lambs to sell! Young lambs to sell!
I never would cry young lambs to sell,
If I'd as much money as I could tell,
I never would cry young lambs to sell.

Trad.

I Doubt

I doubt, I doubt, my fire is out;
My little wife isn't at home;
I'll saddle my dog, and I'll bridle my cat,
And I'll go fetch my little wife home.

Trad.

Little Lamb, Who Made Thee?

Little Lamb who made thee?
Dost thou know who made thee?
Gave thee life and bid thee feed.
By the stream and o'er the mead;
Gave thee clothing of delight,
Softest clothing woolly bright;
Gave thee such a tender voice,
Making all the vales rejoice!
Little Lamb who made thee?
Dost thou know who made thee?
   Little Lamb I'll tell thee,
   Little Lamb I'll tell thee!
   He is called by thy name,
   For he calls himself a Lamb:
   He is meek and he is mild,
   He became a little child:
   I a child and thou a lamb,
   We are called by his name.
   Little Lamb God bless thee.
   Little Lamb God bless thee.

W Blake

Silent C

indictment, muscle, science, scissors, scene, scent, acquit, acquire, yacht…

Do mussels have muscles? If mussels have muscles where are the muscles that mussels have?

Anon.

and see **Fedelma's Song**, on page 46

Silent D

handkerchief, Wednesday, handsome, sandwich, djinn…

from **I Know Where I'm Going**
…Some say he's bad, but I say he's bonny
The fairest of them all
My handsome, win-some Johnny…

Trad.

Silent E

give, like, name, hate, breathe, hope, gave, drive, write, site, grave, bite, hide, vegetable…

This is usually the common silent e. It is worth spending some time showing students the effect of the presence and absence of the ending e on the pronunciation of the penultimate vowel. e.g.
and see **Bird-bath**, on page 13

Short vowel sound	Vowel name sound	with -ing
mat	mate	matting/mating
bed	breathe	bedding/ breathing
sit	site	sitting/ siting
rob	robe	robbing/ robing
cub	cube	cubbing/ cubing

Silent G

gnat, gnaw, gnu, high, phlegm, sign, though, light, reign, campaign, through, foreign, gnash, align…

See **The New Gnu,** on page 55

and see **The Thought I Thought** and **Thoughts Are Birds,** on page 24

and see **Star Light**, on page 85

and see **Goodnight, Sweetheart, Goodnight,** on page 38

Silent H

daughter, heir, honest, hour, ghost, orchid, rhyme, exhaust, choir, yacht, thyme, honour, echo…

Friends, we need to be honest, for this is our hour of honour.

SD Burke

and see **Garry McGarry**, on page 17

and see **Joshua Won the Battle of Jericho,** on page 23

Silent I

friend, business, parliament…

Make new friends,
but keep the old
One is silver and the
others, gold.

Trad.

Silent K

knock, knee, knife, knight, knot, know, knead, knack, knave, kneel, knew, knit, knob, knuckle…

This Old Man

This old man, he played one,
    he played knick knack on my thumb
    with a knick knack paddywhack, give a
    dog a bone,
    this old man went rolling home.
This old man, he played two
    He played knick knack on my shoe
    with a knick knack paddywhack, give a
    dog a bone,
    this old man went rolling home….

Trad.

Now I know what I never knew I knew.

C Beasley.

Nutty Knott

Nutty Knott was not in.
Nutty Knott was out
Knotting knots in netting.
Nutty Knott was out,
But lots of knots
Were in Nutty Knott's knotty netting.

Anon.

A Good Knight

Nighty-night, knight," said one knight to the
other knight the other night. "Nightynight,
knight," answered the other knight the other
night.

Anon.

Bare Knuckled, Knobbly Kneed

Bare knuckled, knobbly kneed
Shortish fellow, fond of mead
At any rate a rare breed
Knobbly kneed, bare knuckle,
Fists fly jaws crackle
Has the knack and doesn't buckle
-Send a big one if you please
(Doesn't know the luck he'll need)
Think I'll put my money
On the knobbly kneed, bare knuckled
Indomitable shortish fellow

SD Burke

Was he a never ever nervous knock kneed
knight, or a never really nervous knock kneed
knight, or a really often really very nervous
knock kneed knight?

SD Burke

and see **Known Unknowns,** on page 33

and see **The Queen of Hearts**, on page 39

Silent L

calf, could, should, would, talk, yolk, half, salmon, balm, walk, calm, folk…

Robin the Bobbin

Robin the Bobbin, the big-bellied Ben,
He eat more meat than fourscore men ;
He eat a cow, he eat a calf,
He eat a butcher and a half ;
He eat a church, he eat a steeple,
He eat the priest and all the people !
    A cow and a calf,
    An ox and a half,
    A church and a steeple,
    And all the good people,
And yet he complained that his stomach
wasn't full.

Trad.

The Calf is Dead

Johnny Armstrong killed a calf.
Peter Henderson got half.
Willy Wilkinson got the head.
Ring the bell, the calf is dead.

Trad.

The Old Man and the Calf

There was an old man,
And he had a calf,
    And that's half.
He took him out of the stall,
And put him on the wall
    And that's all.

Trad.

Silent N

autumn, damn, hymn, solemn, column, condemn…

Merry Autumn

It's all a farce,—these tales they tell
About the breezes sighing,
And moans astir o'er field and dell,
'cause the year is dying.
    Such principles are most absurd,—
I care not who first taught 'em;
There's nothing known to beast or bird
To make a solemn autumn….

PL Dunbar

and see **Three Little Birds**, on page 56

Silent O

leopard, people, colonel, sophomore…

see **Picky People** and **Purple Paper People** on page 12

and see **Phoebe Beebee**, on page 47

Silent P

corps, coup, pneumonia, psalm, psyche, receipt, pumpkin, raspberry, pterodactyl, cupboard…

Old Mother Hubbard

Old Mother Hubbard
Went to her cupboard
To get her poor dog a bone,
But when she got there
The cupboard was bare
And so the poor dog had none…

Trad.

and see **Peter, Pumpkin Eater**, on page 12

Silent S

aisle, debris, island, bourgeois, fracas, apropos, isle, viscount…

Belleisle

At the siege of Belleisle
I was there all the while,
All the while, all the while,
At the siege of Belleisle.

Trad.

Silent T

apostle, fasten, wrestle, ballet, castle, rapport, listen, soften, moisten, thistle, asthma, often*…

Whistle, Daughter, Whistle

"Whistle, daughter, whistle;
Whistle, daughter dear."
"I cannot whistle, mammy,
I cannot whistle clear."
"Whistle, daughter, whistle;
Whistle for a pound."
"I cannot whistle, mammy,
I cannot make a sound."

Trad.

and see **Quiet, Quiet**, on page 66

[*Sometimes a word has a silent letter in one region, class or dialect, but the letter is pronounced in others. The t in '**often**' is a great example.]

Silent U

colleague, guard, guess, tongue, aunt, biscuit, build, circuit, guide, guilt, guitar, dialogue, rogue…

London Bridge is Falling Down

London Bridge is
falling down
Falling down, falling
down,
London Bridge is
falling down
My fair lady.
Build it up with wood
and clay
Wood and clay, wood
and clay
Build it up with wood
and clay
My fair lady…

Trad.

My Aunt Muriel

My Aunt Muriel said, "I wonder,
What would be your favourite number?"
"Dear Aunt Muriel, wait and see,
The one I jump is the one it will be…"
(skipping, 1,2,3,4…)

SD Burke

and see **Biscuit Box**, on page 64

Silent W

answer, sword, two, wrist, wrong, wrench, wrestle, wretched, wrap, wrath, awry, write…

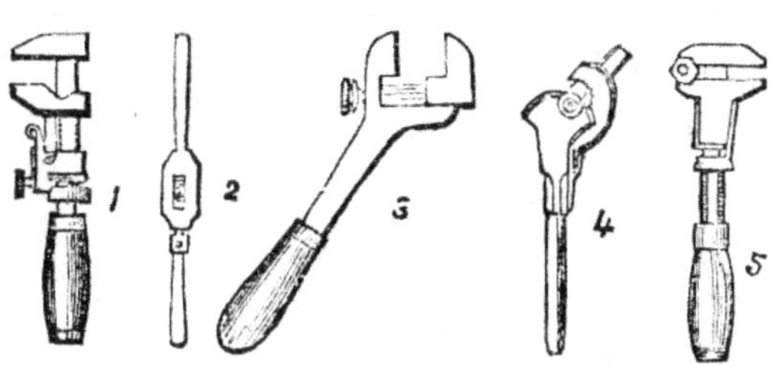

Richard's Wrench

Richard's wretched ratchet wrench
Wouldn't fix the wretched bench
Richard bought it for a song
But the wretched ratchet wrench was wrong.

SD Burke

Wrestling

If rustlers wrestle wrestlers while rustlers rustle rustlers, could rustlers rustle wrestlers while wrestlers wrestle rustlers?

Anon.

and see **Right handed Wright**, on page 30

and see **One One was a Racehorse**, on page 28

and see **The Tudor**, on page 55

Video: https://youtu.be/MKZ1BkhsNA4

Audio: https://audiomack.com/song/we_p/93-sil

	Video	Audio
Wonderful English		

Common Names and Phrases		
Charlotte	John	Connecticut
Eleanor	Thomas	Thailand
Leah	Michael	Thames
Priscilla	Matthew	Carlisle
Violet		Guildford
		Cockburn

~no man is an island~
~to tie the knot~
~an Englishman's home is his castle~
~the pen is mightier than the sword~
~mind your own business~
~a leopard can't change its spots~
~two wrongs don't make a right~
~a friend in need is a friend indeed~

V

COMMON WORDS

Many common words in English are actually quite difficult for new learners to read and pronounce. This is because they are often very old words which have developed, or been fixed with, odd spelling. Mastery of the pronunciation of common words builds confidence and provides a firm basis for further learning.

Sight Words

the	you	I	as	had	other	do	her
of	that	his	by	were	their	make	could
to	was	they	but	all	if	see	go
and	he	at	some	your	will	him	come
a	she	one	what	when	about	not	did
in	for	have	there	up	then	two	my
be	on	this	we	said	them	has	no
is	are	from	can	an	so	look	who
it	with	or	out	which	like	more	over

The above list of 72 of the most common words in English will cover more than half of the words that appear in a normal, non-specialist text. Examples are not provided here as really the whole book is full of examples of these words. Teachers might ask students to locate a verse from parts 1-5 for each common word, in order to see them in context. Students might also usefully create their own short rhyming verse using one or more of the common words as a starting point or recurring word. Being able to use and pronounce sight words in context is essential for further learning.

Referring to Letter Sounds

Teachers use various ways to refer to letter sounds. These strategies may assist, especially when the words are not spelt phonetically, as is the case with many common words.

Letters of the English Alphabet arranged by vowel sound

eɪ	iː	e	ɑɪ	əʊ	uː	ɑː
A	B	F	I	O	Q	R
H	C	L	Y		U	
J	D	M			W	
K	E	N				
	G	S				
	P	X				
	T	Z (zed)				
	V					
	Z (zee)					

The International Alphabet

Alpha	Bravo	Charlie	Delta	Echo	Foxtrot	Golf
Hotel	India	Juliet	Kilo	Lima	Mike	November
Oscar	Papa	Quebec	Romeo	Sierra	Tango	Uniform
Victor	Whiskey	X-Ray	Yankee	Zulu		

An Enlivened Alphabet SD Burke

Aiyah	Bubba	Cutcha	Dow-dow	Eh-heh	Fiefa	Go
Hoo-ha	My-eye (I)	Ja	Kiki	Leddle	Mamma	Ni
Oh-ho	Poppy	*Kiki, Uloo* (Q)	Rara	Sossi	Taitai	Uloo
Viva	Wor-wor	*Eh-he, Kiki, Sossi* (X)	Yaya	Zizzle		

Cardinal Numbers

1	2	3	4	5	6	7	8	9	10	11	12
one	two	three	four	five	six	seven	eight	nine	ten	eleven	twelve

13	30	14	40	15	50	16	60	17	70	18	80
thirteen	thirty	fourteen	forty	fifteen	fifty	sixteen	sixty	seventeen	seventy	eighteen	eighty

Above, the teens are partnered with the tens so students can practise making these very close
sounds, stressing the last syllable for the teens and the first syllable for the tens.

100	1 000	1 000 000	1 000 000 000
one hundred	one thousand	one million	one billion

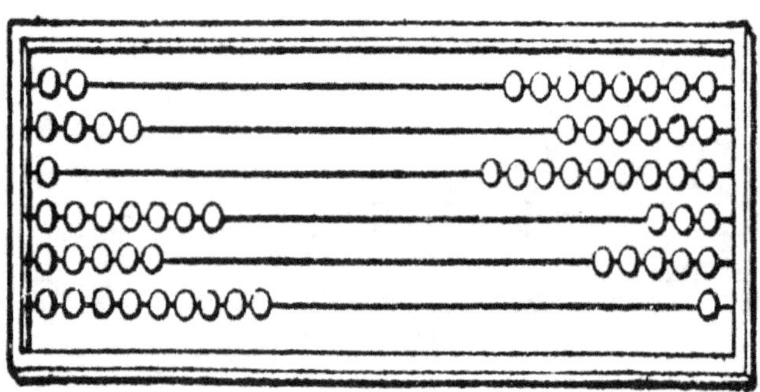

One, He Loves

One, he loves; two, he loves:
Three, he loves, they say;
Four, he loves with all his heart;
Five, he casts away.
Six, he loves; seven, she loves;
Eight, they both love.
Nine, he comes; ten, he tarries;
Eleven, he courts; twelve, he marries.

Trad.

One, Two, Three, Four, Five!

One, two three, four, five
once I caught a fish alive;
six, seven, eight, nine, ten
then I let it go again.
    Why did you let it go?
    Because it bit my finger so.
    Which finger did it bite?
    This little finger on the right.

Trad.

One for sorrow

One for sorrow,
Two for joy,
Three for a girl,
Four for a boy,
Five for silver,
Six for gold,
Seven for a secret
Never to be told.

Trad.

One, Two, Buckle My Shoe

One, two,
Buckle my shoe;
Three, four,
Knock at the door;
Five, six,
Pick up sticks;
Seven, eight,
Lay them straight;
Nine, ten,
A big, fat hen;
Eleven, twelve,
Dig and delve;
Thirteen, fourteen,
Maids a-courting;
Fifteen, sixteen,
Maids in the kitchen;
Seventeen, eighteen,
Maids a-waiting;
Nineteen, twenty,
My plate's empty.

Trad.

Ten in the Bed

There were ten in the bed
And the little one said,
"Roll over! Roll over!"
So they all rolled over
And one fell out
    There were nine in the bed
    And the little one said,
    "Roll over! Roll over!"
    So they all rolled over
    And one fell out…

Trad.

The Ants Go Marching

The ants go marching one by one, hurrah,
hurrah
The ants go marching one by one, hurrah,
hurrah
    The ants go marching one by one,
    The little one stops to suck his thumb
And they all go marching down to the ground
To get out of the rain,
BOOM! BOOM! BOOM! BOOM!
The ants go marching two by two, hurrah,
hurrah
The ants go marching two by two, hurrah,
hurrah,
    The ants go marching two by two,
    The little one stops to tie his shoe…
    The ants go marching three by three
    The little one stops to climb a tree…
    The ants go marching four by four
    The little one stops to shut the door…
    The ants go marching five by five
    The little one stops to take a dive…
    The ants go marching six by six
    The little one stops to pick up sticks…
    The ants go marching seven by seven
    The little one stops to pray to heaven…
    The ants go marching eight by eight
    The little one stops to rollerskate…
    The ants go marching nine by nine
    The little one stops to check the time…
    The ants go marching ten by ten
    The little one stops to shout, "The end!"

Anon.

X Shall Stand for Playmates Ten

X shall stand for playmates ten,
V for five stout stalwart men,
I for one, as I'm alive,
C for a hundred and D for five (hundred),
M for a thousand soldiers true,
And L for fifty, I tell you.

Trad.

Five Currant Buns

Five currant buns in a baker's shop.
Big and round with a cherry on the top,
Along came a boy with a penny one day,
Bought a currant bun and took it away.
    Four currant buns in a baker's shop.
    Big and round with a cherry on the top…

Trad.

Wide-mouthed Waddling Frog

Fourteen Boys at bat-and-ball,
some short and some tall.
Thirteen Sisters all at play,
on a sunshine holiday.
Twelve Huntsmen with horns and hounds,
Hunting over other men's grounds.
Eleven Ships sailing on the main,
Some bound for France, and some for Spain:
(I wish them all safe back again.)
Ten Comets in the sky,
some low and some high.
Nine Peacocks in the air;
I wonder how they all got there:
(You don't know, nor I don't care.)
Eight Joiners in Joiners'-hall,
working with their tools and all.
Seven Lobsters in a dish,
as good as any heart can wish.
Six Beetles against the wall,
close to an old woman's apple-stall.
Five Puppies by our Dog, Ball,
who daily for their breakfast call.
Four Horses stuck in a bog,
Three Monkeys tied to a log.
Two Pudding's-ends that won't choke a dog,
Nor a gaping, wide-mouthed, waddling Frog.

Trad.

Five Fat Sausages

Five fat sausages sizzling in a pan
The grease got hot - and one went "Bang!"
Four fat sausages sizzling in a pan
The grease got hot - and one went "Bang!"
Three fat sausages sizzling in a pan
The grease got hot - and one went "Bang!"
Two fat sausages sizzling in a pan
The grease got hot - and one went "Bang!"
One fat sausage sizzling in a pan
The grease got hot - and it went "Bang!"
No fat sausages frying in a pan.

Trad.

One Potato

One potato, two potato,
three potato - four
Five potato, six potato,
seven potato - more
Eight potato, nine potato,
ten potato – all.

Trad.

Ten Little Fingers

Ten little fingers, ten little toes,
Two little ears and one little nose
Two little eyes that shine so bright
And one little mouth to kiss mother good-
night.

Trad.

Sleep

Nature requires five
Custom gives seven
Laziness takes nine
And Wickedness eleven.

Trad.

Mary's Cherries

One, Two, Three, Four,
Mary's at the cottage door.
Five, Six, Seven, Eight,
Eating cherries off a plate.

Trad.

Forming the Numbers

Around to the left to find my hero
Back to the top, I've made a zero
Downwards stroke, my, that's fun.
Now I've made the number one
Half a heart says 'I love you'
A line, I've made the number two
Around the tree, around the tree
Now I've made the number three.
Down and across and down once more
Now I've made the number four
The hat, the back, the belly- a five
Watch out, it might come alive
Bend down low to pick up sticks
Now I've made the number six.
Across the sky and down from heaven
Now I've made the number seven.
Make an 'S' and close the gate
Now I've made the number eight.
First a circle, then a line
Now I've made the number nine.
One (1) Egg (0) laid my hen
 Now I've made the number ten.

Trad.

and see **This Old Man,** on page 97

and see **Green Grow the Rushes, Oh!** on page 71

and see **The Glutton,** on page 38

and see **Five Little Monkeys,** on page 41

Ordinal Numbers

1st	2nd	3rd	4th	5th	6th	7th	8th	9th	10th	11th	12th
first	second	third	fourth	fifth	sixth	seventh	eighth	ninth	tenth	eleventh	twelfth
13th	16th	20th	23rd	26th	30th	33rd	34th	100th	1000th	1000000th	1000000000th
thirteenth	sixteenth	twentieth	twenty-third	twenty-sixth	thirtieth	thirty-third	thirty-fourth	One hundredth	One thousandth	One millionth	One billionth

The examples in the second line include some of those which students find most difficult

The Twelve Days of Christmas

On the first day of Christmas,
my true love gave to me
a partridge in a pear tree.
On the second day of Christmas
my true love gave to me
    two turtle doves and
    a partridge in a pear tree…
On the twelfth day of Christmas
my true love gave to me
    twelve drummers drumming,
    eleven pipers piping,
    ten lords a leaping
    nine ladies dancing,
    eight maids a milking,
    seven swans a swimming,
    six geese a laying,
    five golden rings,
    four calling birds,
    three French hens,
    two turtle doves
    and a Partridge in a pear tree.

Trad.

Go to Bed First

Go to bed first, a golden purse;
Go to bed second, a golden pheasant;
Go to bed third, a golden bird.

Trad.

First the Worst

First is the worst
Second is the best
Third is the one with the hairy chest…

Anon.

My First is in Snow..

My first is in snow, but not in rain ;
My second in knot, and also in skein ;
My third is in rat, but not in mouse ;
My fourth is in hut, but not in house ;
My fifth in pencil, and also in pen ;
My sixth in slate, and in sponge again.
On my whole, all shod in shining steel,
You glide like a bird, or a boat on its keel,
You curve, you turn, in a thousand ways,
In the merry sport of the winter days.

SE Cassino

The Blind Men and the Elephant

It was six men of Indostan
To learning much inclined
Who went to see the Elephant
(Though all of them were blind),
That each by observation
Might satisfy his mind…

 The *First* approached the Elephant,
 And happening to fall
 Against his broad and sturdy side,
 At once began to bawl:
 "God bless me! but the Elephant
 Is very like a WALL!"

The *Second*, feeling of the tusk,
Cried, "Ho, what have we here,
So very round and smooth and sharp?
To me 'tis mighty clear
This wonder of an Elephant
Is very like a SPEAR!"

 The *Third* approached the animal,
 And happening to take
 The squirming trunk within his hands,
 Thus boldly up and spake:
 "I see," quoth he, "the Elephant
 Is very like a SNAKE!"

The *Fourth* reached out an eager hand,
And felt about the knee
"What most this wondrous beast is like
Is mighty plain," quoth he:
"Tis clear enough the Elephant
Is very like a TREE!"

The *Fifth*, who chanced to touch the ear,
Said: "E'en the blindest man
Can tell what this resembles most;
Deny the fact who can,
This marvel of an Elephant
Is very like a FAN!"

The *Sixth* no sooner had begun
About the beast to grope,
Than seizing on the swinging tail
That fell within his scope,
"I see," quoth he, "the Elephant
Is very like a ROPE!"

 And so these men of Indostan
 Disputed loud and long,
 Each in his own opinion
 Exceeding stiff and strong,
 Though each was partly in the right,
 And all were in the wrong!

So oft in theologic wars,
The disputants, I ween,
Rail on in utter ignorance
Of what each other mean,
And prate about an Elephant
Not one of them has seen!

JG Saxe

Days of the Week

Monday	Tuesday	Wednesday	Thursday	Friday	Saturday	Sunday
the day before yesterday	yesterday	today	tomorrow	the day after to-morrow	The weekend	another day

Tom of Islington

Tom, Tom of Islington,
Married a wife on Sunday,
Brought her home on Monday,
Hired a house on Tuesday,
Fed her well on Wednesday,
Sick was she on Thursday,
Dead was she on Friday,
Sad was Tom on Saturday,
To bury his wife on Sunday.

Trad.

Play Days

How many days has my baby to play?
Saturday, Sunday, Monday,
Tuesday, Wednesday, Thursday, Friday,
Saturday, Sunday, Monday….

Trad.

Solomon Grundy

Solomon Grundy,
Born on a Monday,
Christened on Tuesday,
Married on Wednesday,
Took ill on Thursday,
Worse on Friday,
Died on Saturday,
Buried on Sunday.
That was the end
Of Solomon Grundy.

Trad.

Tommy Snooks and Bessie Brooks

As Tommy Snooks and Bessie Brooks
Were walking out one Sunday;
Says Tommy Snooks to Bessie Brooks,
"Tomorrow will be Monday."

Trad.

Wash on Monday

Wash on Monday,
Iron on Tuesday,
Bake on Wednesday,
Brew on Thursday,
Churn on Friday,
Mend on Saturday,
Meet on Sunday.

Trad.

Video: https://youtu.be/GH2wJI2TxvY
Audio: https://audiomack.com/song/we_p/112-day

Video	Audio

A Gold Ring

On Saturday night
Shall be all my care
To powder my locks
And curl my hair.
On Sunday morning
My love will come in.
When he will marry me
With a gold ring.

Trad.

And see **Sneeze on a Monday,** on page 82

And see **Monday's Child,** on page 22

Months of the Year

1	2	3	4	5	6
January	February	March	April	May	June
7	8	9	10	11	12
July	August	September	October	November	December

Thirty Days Has September

Thirty days has September,
April, June, and November;
February has twenty-eight alone,
All the rest have thirty-one,
Excepting leap-year, that's the time
When February's days are twenty-nine.

Trad.

Video: https://youtu.be/wCbu2UmxY9s
Audio: https://audiomack.com/song/we_p/113-mon

Video	Audio

Cuckoo

Cuckoo, Cuckoo, What do you do?
"In April I open my bill;
In May I sing night and day;
In June I change my tune;
In July away I fly;
In August away I must."

Trad.

The Seasons

Spring	Summer	Autumn	Winter

Child of Spring

I sing to you, O Child of Spring,
A song of praise and life loving
For though we strong and fearless men
Who seek the strength and zeal of ten
Do summer long a goal desire
Which none can reach nor should aspire,
You lie content in fields of youth
To be yourself and not forsooth
Within desires that hero's grasp
To hide behind another's mask.

    Nor will you in Autumn's breeze
    Fall silent like the ageing leaves
    To shed the summer of its gown
    And lay a carpet crimson brown.
    No you will soar in heaven's path
    And to the sky a birdsong laugh
    And while we watch the day decline
    You'll sip the summer-reaped red wine.

Then when the winter chill sets in
We heroes who sought to win
Will die with nought beneath the snow
Yet you will have a seed to show
So when the birds return to sing
You'll still be my child of spring.

D Djurdjevic

As the Days Grow Warm

As the days grow warm my seeds are sprout-
ing
And earth sends high her flowers so fair;
So life springs forth after cold dark winter;
Mother Nature's perfume is in the air.

P Lawrence

And see **Spring Fairy** and **Springtime** on
page 86.

Shall I compare thee to a summer's day?

Shall I compare thee to a summer's day
Thou art more lovely, and more temperate.
Rough winds do shake the darling buds of
May
And Summer's lease hath all too short a
date…

Shakespeare

Down Fall the Leaves

Down fall the leaves
From the old gum trees
Summer heat is drying all the water from the
creeks
Oh, please, send in the breeze
Cool us down and give us shelter
Put our minds at ease

P Lawrence

Summertime

Summertime, and the living is easy.
Fish are jumping, and the cotton is high
Well, your daddy's rich, and your momma's
good-looking
So hush, little Baby, don't you cry…

G Gershwin

And see **A Frog Went Walking**, on page 69

Autumn is Here!

The crickets have ceased their summer song;
The birds sing happily all day long;
The nights are cool, the days are clear;
The bush in its glory! Autumn is here!

P Lawrence

from **Autumn Leaves**

The falling leaves drift by the window
The Autumn leaves of red and gold
I see your lips, the summer kisses
The sunburned hand I used to hold
Since you went away the days grow long
And soon I'll hear old Winter's song
But I miss you most of all, my darling
When Autumn leaves start to fall…

J Prevert & J Mercer

And see **Merry Autumn,** on page 100

Cool Winter

Cool winter, flowing water,
Deep your greens and dark your skies,
Cool winter, flowing water,
Keep me wise and warm inside.

P Lawrence

The Robin

The North wind doth blow and we shall have
snow,
And what will poor robin do then, poor
thing?
He'll sit in a barn and keep himself warm
and hide his head under his wing, poor thing.

Trad.

And see **It's Raining, it's Pouring**, on page
51

And see **Rain, Rain, Go Away**, on page 46

And see **I Hear Thunder**, on page 24

Video: https://youtu.be/UEdotaERDMg	
Audio: https://audiomack.com/song/we_p/114-sea	
Video	Audio

REFERENCES

Aitchison, J. (1976, 1983). *The articulate mammal: An introduction to psycholinguistics.* London, UK: Hutchinson.

Baker, A. (1977, 1981). *Ship or sheep? An intermediate pronunciation course.* Cambridge, UK: CUP.

Binham, P. (1968). *How to say it.* London, UK: Longman.

Byrne, D. (1976). *Teaching oral English.* London, UK: Longman.

Gimson, A.C. (1962, 1989). *An introduction to the pronunciation of English.* London, UK: Edward Arnold.

Grant, T.A. (1968). *Aids to pronunciation in English.* Hong Kong: Universal Publications.

Halliday, M.A.K. (1985). *Spoken and written language.* Melbourne, Vic.: Deakin.

Haycraft, B. (1971). *The teaching of pronunciation: A classroom guide.* London, UK: Longman.

Kimble-Fry, A. (2001). *Perfect pronunciation: A guide for trainers and self-help students.* Sydney, NSW: Clearspeak.

Mortimer, C. (1976). *Stress time.* Cambridge, UK: CUP.

Mortimer, C. (1975). *Sound right!* London, UK: Longman.

Mortimer, C. (1977). *Link-up.* Cambridge, UK: CUP.

Nilsen, D.L.F. & A.P. (1971, 1973). *Pronunciation contrasts in English.* New York, NY: Regents.

Ponsonby, M. (1982, 1992). *How now, brown cow? A course in the pronunciation of English.* Hertfordshire, UK: Phoenix ELT.

Radford, A., Atkinson, M., Britain, D., Clahsen, H. & Spencer, A. (1999, 2009). *Linguistics: An introduction.* Cambridge, UK: CUP.

Swan, M and Smith, B. (2001) Learner English. Cambridge, UK. CUP.

Technical and Further Education (TAFE) NSW (2001). *Teaching pronunciation: A handbook for teachers and trainers.* Sydney, NSW: Department of Education, Training and Youth Affairs.

Trim, J. (1965,1975). *English pronunciation illustrated.* London, UK: CUP.

Underhill, A. (1994, 2005). *Sound foundations: Learning and teaching pronunciation.* Oxford, UK: Macmillan.

Watson, K. (2010). Grammar and Usage: History and Myth. *English in Australia*, Vol.45 No.2. pp.31-37.

LIST OF ILLUSTRATIONS

page
12 [pumpkin]: B. P. Holst (1909) *The Teachers' and Pupils' Cyclopaedia.* Kansas City, KA. The Bufton Book Company.

13 [butter churn]: J. G. Holland (1874) *Scribner's Monthly: an Illustrated Magazine for the People.* New York. Scriber & Company. Vol.VIII p.705

14 [three little kittens]: The Editorial Board of the University Society (1920) *Boys and Girls' Bookshelf.* New York. The University Society. p.139

15 [cat and fiddle]: https://www.wpclipart.com

16 [can of tomatoes]: Hall, G. (1922) *Poco a Poco: An Elementary Direct Method for Learning Spanish.* Hudson, NY. World Book Company.

17 [pigs]: The Editorial Board of the University Society (1920) *Boys and Girls Bookshelf.* New York. The University Society. p.319

18 [boat]: Breasted, J. H. (1914) *Outlines of European History.* Boston, MA. Ginn and Company. p.675

19 [dinosaur]: https://commons.wikimedia.org

20 [fishing]: Sloan, K.E. (1913) *Primary Readers, Second Book.* New York. Macmillan Company. p.148

21 [scales]: Evans, G.C. (1888) *Illustrated History of The United States Mint.* Philadelphia, PA. Author. p.21

22 [woodchuck]: Monteith, J. (1887) *Familiar Animals and their Wild Kindred.* NY. American Book Company. p.84

23 [Jack and Jill]: Mercantile Publishing (1892) *Mother Goose's Nursery Rhymes.* Chicago, IL. Mercantile Publishing & Advertising Co. p.189

24 [drinking]: http://freaky_freya.tripod.com/Drunktionary/E-H.html

25 [lovers]: de Van Natthewman (1903) *Lisle Brevities* . Philadelphia, PA. Henry T. Coates & Company

26 [Jack and Giant]: Lang, A.(ed) (1890) *The Red Fairy Book: Opie collection of children's literature.* Longmans, Green.

27 [Astounding SF Cover]: Campbell, J. (ed) (1939) Astounding Science Fiction. New York. Street and Smith. October 1939

28 [racehorses]: S. G. Goodrich (1885*). The Animal Kingdom Illustrated.* New York. A. J. Johnson & Co. p.588

29 [conversation]: Mercantile Publishing (1892) *Mother Goose's Nursery Rhymes* Chicago, IL. Mercantile Publishing & Advertising Co. p.196

30 [student]: Trowbridge, J.T., Larcom, L. & Hamilton, G. (eds) (1866) *Our Young Folks; An ill. magazine for Boys and Girls.* Boston, MA. Ticknor and Fields. p.195

31 [Mary and lamb]: Leffert, S. (1911) *Land of Play, Verses-Rhymes-Stories* New York. Cuples and Leon Company.

32 [muffin man]: *Punch,* 1892

33 [liberty]: Foster, E.D. (ed.) (1921) *The American Educator (vol. 3)* Chicago, IL. Ralph Durham Company.

34 [pie and birds]: www.worldofmatticus.com

35 [sapsucker]: William Dwight Whitney, W.D. (1911) *The Century Dictionary: An Encyclopedic Lexicon of the English Language.* New York, NY. The Century Co.

38 [woman's face]: MacMillan & Co (1906) *The November Century Magazine.* London, UK. MacMillan and Co. Ltd. Vol. LXXIII p.89

39 [queen of hearts]: Mercantile Publishing (1892) *Mother Goose's Nursery Rhymes* Chicago, IL. Mercantile Publishing & Advertising Co. p.187

40 [bearded man]: Leslie-Judge Co. (nd) *Caricature: Wit and Humor of a Nation in Picture, Sound and Story.* New York. Leslie-Judge Company.

41 [tinker]: Louis Rhead, L. (1912) *Bold Robin Hood and His Outlaw Band.* New York and London, UK. Harper & Brothers p.101

42 [sailors]: Sylvester, C. H. (1909)*Journeys through Bookland, Volume 5.*Chicago, IL. Bellows-Reeve Company.

43 [queen and cat]: Automobile Blue Book Co. (1922) *Official Automobile Blue Book Volume Two.* New York, NY. The Automobile Blue Book Publishing Co. p.198

44 [owl]: Vredenburd, E. & Yeatman Woolf, R. (1913) *Bird Life, Reptiles and Etc.* London, UK. Raphael Tuck and Sons. p.7

45 [train embarkation]: Coggins, H.L. (1906) *Knick Knacks* Philadelphia, PA. The Penn Publishing Company.

46 [girl and umbrella]: University Society Editorial Board (1920) *Boys and Girls Bookshelf* New York. The University Society Vol. 4 p.271

47 [kiss]: Blackburn, H (1889) *Randolph Caldecott, A Personal Memoir* London, UK. Sampson Low, Marston, Searle, and Rivington Limited. p.56

48 [bittern]: Goodrich, S.G.(1859) *Animal Kingdom Illustrated Vol 2* New York, NY. Derby & Jackson.

49 [acrobat]: Berg, A.E. (1883) *The Universal Self-Instructor.* New York. Thomas Kelly. p.346

50 [boys dancing]: University Society Editorial Board (1920) *Boys and Girls Bookshelf* New York. The University Society Vol.4 p.296

51   [couple and mistletoe]: Blackburn, H. (1889) *Randolph Caldecott, A Personal Memoir* London, UK. Sampson Low, Marston, Searle, and Rivington Limited. p.56

52   [kettle]: Long, C.C. (1894) *Home Geography for Primary Grades*. New York American Book Company. p.44

53   [coffee pot]: Kantner, W.C. (1896) *Book of Objects*. Reading, PA. E.H. Rhoads. p.146

54   [fingers]: Whitney, W.D. (1889) *The Century Dictionary and Cyclopedia: An Encyclopedic Lexicon of the English Language*. New York, NY. The Century Co.

55   [rooster]: Goodrich, S.G. (1859) *Animal Kingdom Illustrated Vol 2* New York, NY. Derby & Jackson.

56   [hen and chicks]: Pratt Judson, H & Bender, I.C. (1899) *Graded Literature Readers*. Maynard, Merrill, and Co. p.51

57   [woman and bicycle]: Bryk, N.V. (2011) *American Dress Pattern Catalogs, 1873-1909*. Dearborn, MI. Dover Publications.

60   [cobbler]: Nelson (nd) *My Pretty Present*. New York: Thomas Nelson and Sons.

61   [man and globe]: Houston, E.J. (1891) *The Elements of Physical Geography, for the use of Schools, Academies, and Colleges*. Philadelphia, PA. Eldredge & Brother. p.9

62   [train]: Berg, A.E. (1883) *The Universal Self-Instructor*. New York. Thomas Kelly. p.111

63   [warrior]: Goodrich, S.G. (1885) *The Animal Kingdom Illustrated* New York. A. J. Johnson & Co. p.61

64   [two boys]: Barber, J.W. (1857) *The Handbook of Illustrated Proverbs*. New York, NY. George F. Tuttle. p.47

65   [girl sitting]: University Society Editorial Board (1920) *Boys and Girls Bookshelf* New York. The University Society. Vol 4 p.275

66   [duck]: Kantner, W.C. (1896) *Book of Objects*. Reading, PA. E.H. Rhoads. p.21

67   [sharpening stone]: Kantner, W.C. (1896) *Book of Objects*. Reading, PA. E.H. Rhoads. p.96

68   [flea]: Whitney, W.D. (1889) *The Century Dictionary and Cyclopedia: An Encyclopedic Lexicon of the English Language*. New York, NY. The Century Co. Vol 3 p.2261

69   [frog and mouse]: Mercantile Publishing (1892) *Mother Goose's Nursery Rhymes* Chicago, IL. Mercantile Publishing & Advertising Co. p.96

70   [queen and mirror]: The Brothers Grimm & Rhead, L (1917) *Grimm's Fairy Tales: Stories and Tales of Elves, Goblins, and Fairies* New York. Harper and Brothers. p.257

71   [rushes]: Warren, G.F. (1913) *Elements of Agricul-*

ture. London, UK. MacMillan and Co. Ltd. p.188

72   [man and dog]: Barber, J.W. (1857) *The Handbook of Illustrated Proverbs* New York, NY. George F. Tuttle.

73   [boy and book]: Hall, G (1922) *Poco a Poco: An Elementary Direct Method for Learning Spanish* Hudson, NY. World Book Company.

74   [donkey]: Mee, A & Thompson, H. (eds.) (1912) *The Book of Knowledge* New York, NY. The Grolier Society.

75   [spider]: Finley, J.H.(1917) *Nelson's Perpetual Loose-Leaf Encyclopedia*. New York. Thomas Nelson and Sons. Vol 11 p.375

76   [antelope]: Whitney, W.D. (1889) *The Century Dictionary and Cyclopedia: An Encyclopedic Lexicon of the English Language*. New York, NY. The Century Co. p.5647

77   [priest]: Lane, Rev. C.A. (1901) *Illustrated Notes on English Church History* London,UK. Society for Promoting Christian Knowledge. p.184

78   [princess and frog]: Mee, A & Thompson, H. (eds.) (1912) *The Book of Knowledge* New York, NY. The Grolier Society. Vol 5 p.1316

79   [gravestone]: Lossing, B.J. (1860) *The Pictorial Field-Book of the Revolution*. New York. Harper & Row.

80   [cat]: Harper (1889) *Harper's Young People* New York. Harper and Brothers. Vol. XI No. 526 p.65

81   [asleep in bed]: Beebe, E.M. (1910) *Picture Primer*. New York. American Book Company p.5

82   [sneeze]: Government Printing Office (1895) *The Official Gazette of the United States Patent Office*. Washington, DC. Government Printing Office.

83   [soup]: Kantner, W.C. (1896) *Book of Objects*. Reading, PA. E.H. Rhoads. p.39

84   [fairy]: Gannon,W. (1902) *Mother Goose's Nursery Rhymes, Tales and Jingles* New York. Hurst & Company. p.131

85   [ship]: White, H.A. (1906) *Beginner's History of the US*. New York. American Book Company. p.10

86   [football] Berg, A.E. (1883) *The Universal Self-Instructor*. New York. Thomas Kelly. p.333

87   [swans]: Cuppy, H.A. (ed.) (1895) *Beauties and Wonders of Land and Sea* Springfield, OH. Mast, Crowell & Kirkpatrick. p.260

88   [snowballs]: Blackburn, H (1889) *Randolph Caldecott, A Personal Memoir*. London, UK. Sampson Low, Marston, Searle, and Rivington Limited.

89   [cake]: Mee, A & Thompson, H. (eds.) (1912) *The Book of Knowledge* New York, NY. The Grolier Society. p.3966

90   [rat]: Whitney, W.D. (1889) *The Century Dictionary and Cyclopedia: An Encyclopedic Lexicon of the English*

Language. New York, NY. The Century Co.

91 [robin]: Figuier, L. (1869) *Reptiles and Birds* London, UK.Cassell, Petter & Galpin, p.546

94 [bread]: Hall, G (1922) *Poco a Poco: An Elementary Direct Method for Learning Spanish* Hudson, NY. World Book Company.

94 [lamb]: https://t4.ftcdn.net

95 [mussel]: Buel P. Colton, B.P. (1903) *Zoology: Descriptive and Practical* Boston, MA. D.C. Heath & Co. p.124

95 [bowing]: Klugh, M. (1909) *Tales from the Far North* Chicago, IL. A. Flanagan Company.

95 [birdbath]: Bradbury & Evans (1851) *The Art Journal: The Industry of All Nations Illustrated Catalogue* London, UK. Bradbury and Evans.

96 [gnu]: Goodrich, S.G. (1885) *The Animal Kingdom Illustrated* New York. A. J. Johnson & Co. p.529

96 [fort]: *Encyclopaedia Britannica* (1910) *(11th ed., vol. 5)* New York, NY. The Encyclopaedia Britannica Company.

96 [boys running]: Sylvester, C.H. (1909) *Journeys Through Bookland* Chicago, IL. Bellows-Reeve Company. Vol.VI p.347

97 [knight]: Colby, F.M. (1899) *Outlines of General History.* New York. American Book Company. p.267

98 [man and calf]: The Editorial Board of the University Society. (1920) *Boys and Girls Bookshelf*. New York, NY. The University Society.

98 [girl and leaves]: Hall, G (1922) *Poco a Poco: An Elementary Direct Method for Learning Spanish* Hudson, NY. World Book Company

99 [leopard]: Goodrich, S.G. (1885) *The Animal Kingdom Illustrated* New York. A. J. Johnson & Co. p.264

99 [Mother Hubbard]: Sylvester, C.H.(1909) *Journeys Through Bookland* Chicago, IL.Bellows-Reeve Company.Vol.I p.28

99 [boat and island]: Miller, O.B. (1920) *The Treasure Chest of My Bookhouse* Chicago, IL. The Bookhouse for Children. Vol.IV p.17

100 [mother and children]: The Editorial Board of the University Society. (1920) *Boys and Girls Bookshelf* New York, NY. The University Society.

100 [singer]: Dorado, C.M. (1917) *España Pintoresca: The Life and Customs of Spain in Story and Legend* Boston, MA. Ginn & Company.

101 [wrenches]: Williams, H.L. (1889) *The World's Cyclopedia* New York. World Manufacturing Co. p.444

101 [knot]: Davison, A. (1910) *Health Lessons* New York. American Book Company. p.237

104 [telescope]: Kantner, W.C. (1896) *Book of Objects.* Reading, PA. E.H. Rhoads. p.130

105 [abacus]: Leonard-Stuart, C. (1912) *Everybody's Cyclopedia* New York. Syndicate Publishing Company.

106 [ant]: Bergen, J.Y. (1896) *Elements of Botany* Boston, MA. Ginn & Company.

109 [ice skating]: Finley, J.H. (1917) *Nelson's Perpetual Loose-Leaf Encyclopedia* New York. Thomas Nelson and Sons Vol. 11 p.239

110 [elephant]: Goodrich, S.G. (1885) The Animal Kingdom Illustrated. New York. A. J. Johnson & Co. p.629

111 [ring]: (Editor's own ring, purchased secondhand in Kilkenny, Ireland in 2001.)

111 [cuckoo]: Chambers, W&R. (1881) *Encyclopaedia - A Dictionary of Universal Knowledge for the People* Philadelphia, PA. J. B. Lippincott & Co.

112 [maypole]: Harper (1871) *Harper's New Monthly Magazine* New York, NY. Harper & Brothers.

112 [children on beach]: Leffert, S.T. (1911) *Land of Play, Verses-Rhymes-Stories* New York. Cuples and Leon Company.

113 [autumn orchard]: The Editorial Board of the University Society. (1920) *Boys and Girls Bookshelf* New York, NY. The University Society.

113 [winter valley]: Longfellow, H.W. (1899) *The Poetical Works of Henry Wadsworth Longfellow* New York, NY. Houghton, Mifflin and Company. p.124

INDEX

A

A Beetle and a Broom Straw 86
A dish of fish 20
A Fella 31
A Fly and a Flea in a Flue 68
A Frog Went Walking 69
A Gold Ring 113
A Good Knight 97
a hundred hands 73
a lady sweet and kind 38
A Sailor Went to Sea 18
A synonym for cinnamon 33
Ah, the Moon! 39
Air hair lair 43
All a Row 73
All the world is queer 49, 66
Amidst the Mists 90
An antelope 76
An Earthly Hand 18
Ann and Andy's anniversary 45
Any noise annoys an oyster 50
Are you Sleeping? 34, 81
As a beauty I'm not a great star 39
As the Days Grow Warm 114
Autumn is Here! 115
Autumn Leaves 115

B

Baa Baa Black Sheep 13
Baby Dear 49
Bake big batches 61
Bandy Legs 42, 72
Be a Clown 52
Bees 87
Belleisle 99
Bernie Burke 44
Betty Botter 13
Betty Pringle's Pig 17
Big black bugs 60
Birches 63
Biscuit Box 64
Bitter Biting Bittern 48
Blair's all black bike 60
Bless the Earth 60
Blind as a Bat 13
Blow the Man Down 60

Blue Girl Beer 60
Blue glue gun 70
Bobby Shaftoe 13
Bonnie B 13
Brilliant Boring Brian 61
Bring a Plate 77
Brother from another mother 25, 41
Brown Bread 61
Brussel Sprouts 84
Bryan O'Lin 61
bucket of bug blood 40
Bunch of blue ribbons 60
Busy buzzing bumble bees 19
Bye Baby Bunting 34

C

can be counted 76
Car Park 39
Casual clothes 21
Celibate celebrant 61
Certified certificates 44
Child of Spring 114
Chook Book 56
Chop shops 53
Christmas cracker wrapper 63
Circle Song 18
Clap Your Hands 62
Clean clams 62
Click go the Shears 62
Climbing over Rocky Mountains 21
Close Family 25
Cobbler, cobbler 60
Come Follow 26
Come With Me 34
Come, Let's to Bed 81
Connor McCracken 63
Cool Winter 115
Copper Bottom? 32
Cows Eat Wheat 91
cricket critic 63
Cuckoo 113
Cut Thistles in May 25

D

Dan, Dan 45
Ddodd 15
dewdrop 67

Did Doug dig Dick's garden 15
Diddle Diddle Dumpling.............................. 77
Do mussels have muscles? 95
Doctor Foster 41
Doctor! 65
Double bubble gum 40
Down Fall the Leaves................................ 114
drowsy ducks and drakes 67
Dull Dark Dock 16, 53

E

Early to bed 19
Earth Lag 72
Earthside 79
East Fife: Four 26
Elizabeth's birthday 24
Ella Ella Ate 42
Enjoy 50
Every day's a little death 24
Evil Vanquished 15

F

Fat frogs flying past fast 68
Father Placid 77
Fed Ex 64
Fedelma's Song 46
Fee Fie Fo Fum.. 26
field of fitches 22
Fingers and Toes 54
Firenze 22
First the Worst 110
Fish and chips and vinegar 48
Five Currant Buns 108
Five fat friars 69
Five Fat Sausages 108
Five Little Monkeys.............................. 42, 74
Five Little Speckled Frogs 83
Five of Seven 27
Five Plump Peas.. 12
Flabby friars 69
Fleas.. 68
For a Bride 24
For Want of a Nail 76
Four score and seven................................ 26
Fred fed Ted 69
Fred Threlfall 88
Free, free, free 69
Fresh Baked Bread 94
Fresh French 69
Fresh fried fish 69

Friends, we need to be honest 96
From a Jack to a King 69
From the Earth 47
Frown Down 52
Frying Pan Theology 69
Full Kettle 14
Fuzzy Wuzzy.. 19

G

Garry McGarry 17
Georgie Porgie 23
Giddy Goat 17
Give Me Blessings 17
Glass 70
go for a gopher.. 26
Go to bed first 44, 110
Go to Sleep My Baby 81
Gobbling gargoyles 60
God in the Quad 53
Going to the Zoo 19
Good Morning 56
Good night, sleep tight.............................. 38
Goodnight, Sweetheart, goodnight 38
Great gray goats 71
Greek grape growers 71
Green glass globes.................................... 70
Green grow the rushes 71
Grey Goose and Grey Gander.................... 41
groundhog 71

H

had had 29, 45
Hands on Shoulders 73
Happy Birthday.............................. 12, 29, 79
Happy Birthday, Sun and Moon 79
Hark hark the dogs do bark 39
Have You Ever? 42
He Couldn't 76
He has a nice hat 29
He That Would Thrive 88
He threw three balls 88
He who has ears 49
Hector Protector 65
Here is the church 47
Here we go 'round the mulberry bush 28
Hey Didde Diddle 15
Hey, Ho 50
Hickory Dickory Dock................................ 16
Horsie, Horsie.. 62
Hot cross buns 53

How can I be happy 29
How do you do? 55
How many cars would a car park park 39
How many cookies 56
How many yaks 35
How much is that doggie in the window?............17
How much oil 50
How now brown cow? 52
Huck and Tom 21
Hum, Hem, Him 29
Humpty Dumpty 40, 51

I

I Doubt 94
I dropped it 67
I fry 69
I had a little nut tree 40, 89
I Have a Dream 16
I Have a Little Dreidel 67
I Hear Thunder 24
I hope I will be happy 29
I Know Where I'm Going...........................95
I like selfless shellfish 20
I Love Sixpence 75
I Love to Have a Beer with Duncan.................74
I really like 31
I Saw Esau..51
I see the moon..32
I spy 83
I think I'd like 24
I Was Only Nineteen 65
I Wish...20
I'd rather wear roses 30
I'm a Little Teapot....................................52
I've Danced With a Man 75
If all the Land 74
If All the Seas 71
If I Had a Donkey 74
If two witches...28
imaginary menagerie manager 23
In Hertford...29
Incy Wincy Spider...............................75, 83
Iranian Uranium 33
Irish Wristwatch 30
It would be handy....................................29
It's Raining, it's Pouring.........................51, 90
Ivan's Wives 27

J

Jack and Jill...23

Jack Be Nimble.......................................23
Jack Sprat 45, 84
Jack Straw's Castle 86
Jenny jumped..23
Jenny Who? 23
Jim Along Josie 23
Joshua won the battle of Jericho 23
Joy to the World......................................50
Just Like You...35

K

Kind Hearts..73
King Arthur's Passing 15
Kitty caught a kitten 16
Known Unknowns 33
Kubla Khan 21

L

Larry Hurley 44
Lavender's blue.......................................31
Lazy Zvesdan 19
Leisure...43
Lesser leather 42
Life is But a Melon 68
Lines and Squares 43
Little Cock Sparrow..................................83
Little Donkey 74
little fishy 63
Little Lamb, Who Made Thee?.......................94
Little Miss Muffett 26
Little Mousey Brown 52
Little Peter Rabbit....................................68
Little Polly Flinders 41
Little red lorry..31
Little Snow White 70
Lock and Key 16
Lock Up Your Stock 53
Lolly Legs Eleven 72
London Bridge is Falling Down 100
Lord of the Dance 75
Louis Pasteur...57
Loyal Roy 50
Lucy Locket..41
Lydia 49

M

Make new friends 96
Many an anemone....................................33
Many Legs 72
Mary Had a Little Lamb..............................31

Mary Mac 32
Merry Autumn 98
Michael Finnigan... 48
minimum of cinnamon...................................... 32
Miss Polly Had a Dolly 65
Mister!... 41, 44
Mix a pancake 16
Mo Mi Mo.. 32
Mockingbird... 44
Monday's Child 22
Money and the Mare 32
Moses Supposes 54
My Aunt Muriel... 100
My Black Hen 42
My Bonnie lies over the ocean 61
My First is in Snow 111
My Friend Gladys... 45
My Hat... 29
My Paddle's Clean and Bright 48
My racecar.. 30
My Story's Ended.. 73

N

Near an ear... 49
New York 33, 51
Nine nice night nurses 33
Ninety nine nuns 33
North Perth 24
North, South, East, West..................................... 85
Nose, Nose, Jolly Red Nose 19
Not a Beauty 39
Not everything that can be counted counts.............. 16
Not the Cough 26
not the nun I know 33
Nothing is worth 24
Now I know.. 97
Nuts in May 90
Nutty Knott 97

O

Oats peas beans.. 54
odd socks box 64
Oh what a tangled web we weave 28
Oh What a To Do... 14
Old Chairs to Mend 63, 73
Old King Cole.. 54
Old Mother Hubbard 99
Old oily Ollie 50
old woman who swallowed a fly. 87
On Forgiveness... 26

one flew over the cuckoo's nest 85
One for sorrow 106
One man went to mow.. 32
One One was a Racehorse 28
One Potato 108
One, He Loves 106
One, Two, Buckle My Shoe............................... 107
One, Two, Three, Four, Five! 106
Only One Mother 67
Oonagh's Plaits 77
Oonagh's Plan... 88
Our House 52
our presence... 78
Oyster Stew.. 50

P

Paddle Little Ducks 64
Painful James 46
Pairs or Pears 91
Pat a Cake 46
Paul Plymouth.. 77
Pease Porridge Hot 12, 53
Pen, Pineapple, Apple, Pen................................ 12
Penny, penny.. 76
Person from Tring... 34
Peter Piper 12, 65
Peter, Pumpkin Eater 12
Phoebe Beebee 47
pick up sticks... 64
Picky People.. 12
Pirate's Private Property 78
Play Days 112
Polly Put the Kettle On 31
Polly Wolly Doodle 31
Polonius to Laertes... 25
Pope Sixtus 64
Post Asia.. 21
Practically Perfect.. 78
Pretty Kitty Creighton 14
Proper Cup of Coffee.................................... 53, 78
Purple Paper People 12
Pussy Cat, Pussy Cat... 43

Q

Queen Caroline 66
Quick kiss 66
Quiet, Quiet... 66

R

Rain, rain, go away 46

Rebecca MacGregor 65
Red leather, yellow leather 25
Restless, hissing tongues 18
Rhyme of the Ancient Mariner....................81
Rhys watched Ross 30
Richard's Wrench 101
Right-handed Wright 30
Ring-a-Rosies 54
Ripe white wheat reapers 30
Roberta ran rings 30
Robin the Bobbin 98
Rock a bye, Baby 13
Rockin' robin 91
Roman nose 33
Rotten Eggs 72
Round and round the rugged rocks 30
Round the garden 43
Row, Row, Row Your Boat....................30, 54
Roy Rogers 30
Rub a dub dub 40
Run Rabbit 30

S

Saint Swithin's Day 87
Sally go 'round the sun.............................18
Say This 25
Scissors sizzle 19
Sea Fever 18, 85
See a Pin 12
Seventy seven benevolent elephants 42
Shall I compare thee to a summer's day? 114
She Sells 20
Shoo! Fly 20, 68
Shortning bread 20
Shropshire South 20
Shut the Shutter 40
Simon says 18
Sing a Song of Sixpence 34
Singing Along 34
Sippity Sup 40
Sir Bedivere 38
Sir Gawain and the Green Knight 70
Six crisp snacks 63
Six Little Ducks 66
Six slick slimy snails 81
Skillful Smith, the Skatepark Hero 80
Skip to my Lou 80
Sleep..108
Sleep Baby, Sleep 81
Slip, slop, slap 81

Sneeze on a Monday 82
Snowflakes 82
Snug as a bug in a rug 17
Solomon Grundy....................................112
Split Pea Broth 83
Spring Fairy 84
Springtime 34, 84
St Ives 27
Stand clear of the closing doors 62
star-cross'd lovers 26
Sticks and stones................................64, 85
String string 86
strong stocky soccer striker 86
Stuck Fast 85
Stupid superstition 85
Summertime 115
Sunrise, sunset 18
Swan Swam 87
Swanee 87
Swing Low, Sweet Chariot 87
Swing Me Over the Water...........................87
Swinging on a Star 39

T

Teddy Bear 42
Ten Green Bottles 71
Ten in the Bed 107
Ten Little Fingers 108
The Ant and the Elephant 76
The Ants Go Marching.............................107
The Arrow 38
The Arrow and the Song............................43
The Aunts 76
The best breath test 42
The best chips 22
The Bird's Nest 83
The Blind Men and the Elephant 111
The Boy of Baghdad 45
The Brewer Tour 57
The British bloke's 61
The Calf is Dead 98
The Canner..16, 45
The Cannibal 33
The Cat Spat 80
The Clock 62
The Curate 57
The Duchess 47
The Dumplings..77
The Elephone 26
The Empty Glass......................................70

The Farmer in the Dell 22
The Felt I Felt 26
the first day of Christmas 89
The Fisher Named Fischer 20
The fishwife 48
The Forest Stands 47
The Frog Prince 78
The Genesis Of The Butterfly 68
The Glutton 38
The Groat 54
The Gypsies 23
The handsome hero 29
The Happy Wanderer 27
The Hippopotamus 40
The House that Jack Built 25
The instinct of an extinct insect 65
the king's a great man 71
The Lion and the Unicorn 52
The lips, the teeth, the tip of the tongue 14
The Little Laugh 31
The Lonely Goatherd 35
The Maiden of Glenmalure 57
The Man in Thessaly 80
The Man of Bengal 51
The Mathematician of Trinity 48
The Measure of Treasure 21
the Mongol hordes 51
The Monkeys and the Crocodile 82
The Muffin Man 32
The Need of Needles 33
The New Gnu 55
the night before Christmas 52
The Old Man and the Calf 98
The Old Man of Dunoon 55
The Old Man of Peru 55
The Old Man of Vancouver 44
The Old Man with a Beard 49
The only thing we have to fear 49
The Pied Piper 90
The Pieman 31
The Queen of Hearts 39, 90
The rain in Spain 46
The Rainy Day 49
The Rhyme of the Ancient Mariner 67
The Robin 115
The sixth sick sheik's 20
The Sneeze 82
The Soldier 31
The Square Triangle 66
The Student Named Essar 41

The Teacher 46
The Thought I Thought 24
The Three Foxes 64
The Three Little Kittens 14
The Three Ravens 15, 88
The Tide in the River 41
The Train 62
The Tudor 35, 55
The Twelve Days of Christmas 110
The Twister of Twists 91
The Tyger 14
The Valiant Venusians 27
The Walrus and the Carpenter 34
The Walrus and the Oysters 47
The Water 28
The Wild Colonial Boy 50
The Windhover 51
The Witches 22
The Woodchuck 22
The Young Fellow From Perth 79
The Young Fellow Named Weir 49
The Young Girl of West Ham 45
The Young Lady of Lynn 48
The Young Lady of Riga 38
Theophilus Thistle 88
Theo's throat 88
There is a Lady 38
There is a Stone 85
There Was a Crooked Man 56, 63
There was a Little Turtle 82
There was an old woman who swallowed a fly 38, 87
There Were Five in the Bed 54
There, They're and Their 43
There's a Hole in the Bucket 67, 86
Thirty Days Has September 113
This is the Way 89
This Little Froggy 69
This Little Piggy 17
This Old Man 97
Thoughts Are Birds 24
Thousands 24
Three blind mice 38
three drops of drink 67
three free throws 88
Three grey geese 71
Three Little Birds 56
Three Young Rats 88
Tinker, Tailor 41
To Market 17
To Morrow 54

Tom of Islington 112
Tom Thumb.......................................29
Tommy Snooks and Bessie Brooks 112
Tommy Trot.......................................86
Too Wise...19
Tour of the Moor 57
Trick or Treat 89
Tricky Tristan 89
Truly rural 30
Turkey in the Straw.............................86
Tweedledum and Tweedledee 91
Twice Two 91
Twinkle, Twinkle, Little Star 91
Two and Two 55
Two cats of Kilkenny............................16

U

Under the Earth 44, 79
Unjust...40
Until Disproven.................................84
Upon the Stair 43

W

War No More 51
Wash on Monday.............................112
Wash the dishes 20
Watchers Watching.............................22
We wish you a merry Christmas 63
We Wish You a Merry Christmas.............56
What are Little Boys Made of? 50, 82
What Tate Ate 46
Where are you going to 20, 78
Where has my little dog gone? 28
Where is thumbkin?............................43
Where the Dwarven Dwell 15

Where You There?........................89
Whereat with blade 60
Whether the weather......................25
Whistle, Daughter, Whistle 100
Why Willy? 28
Wide-mouthed Waddling Frog.............108
Widespread rioting........................84
Will you, William?........................28
Willie Sent Millicent......................76
Willie's really weary.......................30
Willy's real rear wheel 31
winter of our discontent 76
Wise Old Owl.............................44
Wooden Heart.............................56
World wide web...........................28
Wrestling 101
Wynken, Blynken and Nod 74

X

X Shall Stand for Playmates Ten 108
Xanadu...................................29

Y

Y's a crooked letter.......................19
Yellow Bellied Sapsucker 35
Yoda.....................................35
You are my Sunshine 20
You cannae hand a man...................45
You never count your money..............35
You're a Grand old Flag 68
Young Lambs to Sell 35, 94

Z

Zachary the Dinosaur 19

ABOUT THE AUTHOR

Sean David Burke is an educator and writer based in Western Australia.

Sean's experience includes high school teaching, many years in senior ESL, a year in Italy teaching English to students of all ages, adult prison and university teaching and seven years as a Steiner/Waldorf primary class teacher.

Sean believes that both education and society progress through the collegial freedom and responsibility teachers and other artists have for their work. He is available to present workshops to staff groups on a wide range of topics; see www.earthsideeducation.com

Sean lives with his partner, Andrea and they are blessed with their now adult children: Thomas, Genevieve and Bonnie.

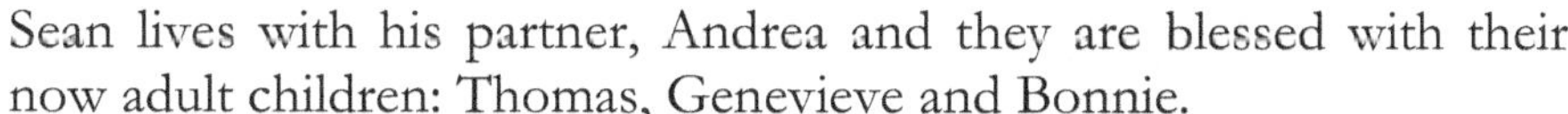

How can I really light the fire for my students?

Lighting the Literacy Fire is the perfect gift for a young primary teacher starting out, or for the older, experienced teacher who is looking for some fresh ideas. Here, Sean has collected his seven years of experience in the Steiner Waldorf system and explained a useful relational teaching approach in a way that teachers in all schools will find accessible and enjoyable.

The book covers the prerequisites for learning, describes approaches for different ages with examples and useful materials, and discusses the organisational structures within which inspirational teaching can best take place.

A portion of the profits from the sale of these and Sean's other books goes to the India Sponsorship Committee, which provides education to the children of construction labourers in Pune and other cities in India. http://www.ashanet.org/projects/project-view.php?p=932